We've Got to Try

Also by
Beto O'Rourke

Dealing Death and Drugs
(with Susie Byrd)

Beto O'Rourke

HOW *the* FIGHT *for* VOTING RIGHTS
MAKES EVERYTHING ELSE POSSIBLE

We've Got to Try

FLATIRON
BOOKS
NEW YORK

www.flatironbooks.com

Designed by Devan Norman

The Library of Congress Cataloging-in-Publication Data is available upon request.

ISBN 978-1-250-85245-8 (hardcover)
ISBN 978-1-250-85247-2 (ebook)

Our books may be purchased in bulk for promotional, educational, or business use. Please contact your local bookseller or the Macmillan Corporate and Premium Sales Department at 1-800-221-7945, extension 5442, or by email at MacmillanSpecialMarkets@macmillan.com.

First Edition: 2022

10 9 8 7 6 5 4 3 2 1

For Lawrence Nixon and all who fight for the right to vote,
whatever the odds

Contents

CONTENTS

PART III

VIII

We've Got to Try

Prologue

It was November 1886, just after midnight, and the poll workers in Washington County knew something was wrong as soon as Dewees Bolton walked into the Flewellyn precinct.

Voting had concluded and now counting by official election workers was well underway. So it was an odd time for a stranger to burst through the door, especially one whose face was covered by a handkerchief.

Bolton was also wearing a slicker—a yellow oilproof coat—that further disguised his appearance.

And he had a gun.

This wasn't the first time a Black polling location in Washington County had been attacked. Two years earlier, three Black elections officials had been murdered at a polling location ten miles away. And earlier this night, ballot boxes in the area had been stolen.

To the poll workers in Flewellyn, it would have been clear that a violent, organized plot to rig the election was underway.

So when the armed intruder made for the ballot box in a blatant attempt to destroy the votes before the count could be finished in this heavily Black precinct, the poll workers decided to fight back—to defend democracy.

In the struggle, one of them shot and killed Bolton.

It was later revealed that the intruder was in fact a member of a gang of ballot thieves organized by the "People's Party" of Washington County, an offshoot of a movement that had recently burst onto the scene in the former Confederacy hoping to "redeem" communities from Black political participation. Their goal, in other words, was to keep the political system entirely white, even after slavery had been abolished. And violence was the primary tool they used to accomplish that objective.

Yet despite the clear evidence that it was the People's Party that brought danger to Washington County that night, the only people arrested in connection with the events were those who stopped Bolton from stealing the ballot boxes.

Within a week of the election, the sheriff apprehended eight African American men for Bolton's death. But within a month, and before a court could rule on whether or not they were guilty, an "unidentified" group of men broke into the jail where they were being held, abducted three of the prisoners, and took them to Sandy Creek, about a mile outside of town.

There, the three prisoners—Shad Felder, Alfred Jones, and Stewart Jones—were hanged. While some attempted to claim that the lynchings were directed by unknown members of the Klan, it soon became clear that the plot to steal the election—and perhaps the plan to kill the poll workers—was led by the man at the top of the countywide ticket, incumbent county judge Lafayette Kirk.

After visiting the Flewellyn polling location on Election Night, Kirk telegraphed Bolton with the message: "Things here look gloomy; do your work." It was only after receiving those instructions that Bolton arrived with his handkerchief, slicker, and gun to steal the votes.

Nevertheless, the popular press blamed the hangings not on Kirk or the terrorists of the People's Party but on the party that had been attacked in the first place. The *Galveston News* claimed the lynchings were the effect of "incendiary speeches" made by Republican candidates. "While all good citizens regret the hanging," the paper wrote, "they cannot but think that tardy justice was done."

The newspaper in Brenham, the county seat, agreed and argued that the lynchings were conducted with the utmost gentility.

> The hanging of these negroes by a mob is an occurrence to be regretted, but it was brought on by the very men who professed to have the greatest friendship for the negro. . . . The negroes were scientifically hanged with new grass ropes. . . . The bodies were cut down and hauled to town. . . . New drawers, undershirts, and nice shrouds were purchased and good coffins procured . . . after which they were turned over to their friends and relatives, who took them to their former homes near Flewellen for burial.

Though Kirk would be brought to trial by the United States attorney in Austin, the case against the leader of the Washington County election thieves never stood much of a chance.

To start with, Kirk's defense was provided pro bono by former Texas governor John Ireland. Also accompanying Kirk during the trial was sitting U.S. senator Richard Coke. There would be no mistaking where the real power in Texas stood, regardless of the facts of the case.

The attorney for the three lynched poll workers laid out the details of the ballot-theft plot and made the case that their murders were an effort to silence the witnesses to the original crime. He insisted that they were killed because they were the only ones who could provide the necessary incriminating testimony about Judge Kirk's role in the plot. But whatever the evidence, the jury took the side of Kirk and the powerful men who stood with him.

After just three days of testimony and deliberations, they found Kirk innocent.

The failure to hold the ringleaders accountable not only made a mockery of the rule of law but also sent a chilling message to those who might still believe in free and fair elections: Not here. Not now. Not yet.

I first heard this story as I was working on voting rights in Texas in January 2021 with a group of new volunteers. We had started Powered by People the year before to register voters across the state and fight for the full franchise for all eligible citizens. More than twenty thousand volunteers eventually signed up, registering hundreds of thousands of voters and convening conversations on voting rights across the state, from some of the smallest rural counties to the biggest cities in Texas. These new recruits were stepping up to join the effort.

I did my best to make the case that the work I was asking them to do was urgent. I told them that since 2013, more than 750 polling locations had been closed across Texas—far more than in any other state, and most of them were concentrated in the fastest-growing Black and Latino neighborhoods.

I shared that a panel of three federal judges, two of whom were appointed by Republican presidents, described our congressional districts as a "racial gerrymander" for drawing voters of color out of competitive districts to diminish the power of their vote.

And I cataloged other extreme measures taken in Texas since the Voting Rights Act was stripped of much of its power to protect the right to vote by the Supreme Court's 2013 *Shelby v. Holder* decision, keeping millions from participating in our democracy.

I then asked them, "How can we get Texans, especially young Texans, to understand the stakes when it comes to voting rights?"

Tayhlor Coleman, a young volunteer whom I was meeting for the first time, was the first to respond.

"Something that really helped me view the stakes more plainly was getting grounded in the proud history of Black Texans' place in the fight for the right to vote, beginning right after emancipation.

"By learning that history," she continued, "I was able to recognize the direct through line to the fights we are still having over voting rights, suppression, and disenfranchisement today.

"A great example is what happened in Washington County in 1886. I'm reading the Senate testimony following the 'election outrage' there and it reminds me a lot of what just happened on January 6."

She shared with us some of the story, which it turns out was personal for her.

Shad Felder—one of the three men hanged by the mob—was a relative of hers.

Shad Felder is not a household name, but he should be. The past is easily forgotten, but the urgent truth of our history is all around us if we choose to listen. Tayhlor carried the hurt of her family's betrayal to that meeting of volunteers. She wanted me to understand that her story belonged to all of us. That bitter, life-and-death fight for democracy that took place in 1886 was not some relic of the past but an urgent warning for our future.

Meeting Tayhlor, listening to her story, knowing that, more than a century after one of her ancestors had been killed for defending the franchise, she was willing to do her part to fight for it, made me think differently about the work we were doing. I no longer saw the state's effort to disenfranchise millions of Texans in the aftermath of *Shelby* as an anomaly. It was a return to the way things used to be and the way they will be for the foreseeable future unless we do something about it.

The lessons of our history clearly show us that fair elections—where all eligible citizens are able to freely cast their votes without intimidation, suppression, or obstruction—have always been the exception, not the rule.

That exception—the forty-eight years between the passage of the Voting Rights Act in 1965 and its undoing in *Shelby* in 2013—was a golden age. While far from perfect—Texas was found in violation of the Voting Rights Act in every decade following its signing—this era of federal voting rights protection gave our democracy a chance to include an increasingly diverse array of voices and perspectives, reflected in a government that slowly began to resemble the electorate it purported to represent.

If history confirms that the right to vote was always under threat, sometimes violently so, it might also offer a guide for how we could overcome these threats, and make the exception of free and fair elections the new rule. I was looking for lessons to help me understand the consequences of the choice before us now: stand up and fight for democracy or stand back and hope that someone else will do it for us.

———

The "Texas Election Outrage" of 1886, as the Washington County violence came to be known, was the focus of a federal inquiry in both the U.S. Senate and House of Representatives. The investigations documented the complete impunity with which white terrorists could steal elections and kill Black citizens. They also looked at widespread instances of voter suppression and intimidation throughout Texas and much of the South that effectively denied African Americans the franchise.

Poll taxes and literacy tests, for example, vastly reduced Black voter participation while leaving white voters untouched thanks to "grandfather clauses," which exempted any man whose grandfather had been a voter from these new restrictions. (Given that slavery had been abolished less than a generation earlier in Texas, only white men qualified.)

The findings prompted Representative Henry Cabot Lodge and Senator George Frisbie Hoar, both of Massachusetts, to introduce legislation in 1890 to provide federal oversight and intervention in the elections administered by the states. The goal was to protect the franchise for Black voters and prevent the kind of political terrorism and Jim Crow election practices that had come to dominate Washington and other southeast Texas counties from becoming the norm in the rest of Texas and throughout the former Confederacy.

The Federal Elections Bill (known by its critics as the Lodge Force Bill) was the most significant attempt at guaranteeing the franchise since the adoption of the Fourteenth and Fifteenth Amendments. A bill of this scope would not be matched again in federal legislation until Lyndon Johnson signed the Voting Rights Act of 1965 into law.

The House passed the measure in December 1890, on a strict party-line vote, and Senator Hoar felt optimistic about its prospects in the upper chamber. But before a final vote could be taken, Senate Democrats initiated a filibuster that temporarily prevented action on the bill.

The Republicans had the numbers to overcome the filibuster and proceed with passage. They had recently won majorities in the House and Senate, and, with the election of Benjamin Harrison in 1888, controlled the presidency, too. In fact, Harrison and congressional Republicans had campaigned on securing voting rights, especially for the Black targets of voter suppression efforts in the South.

There was also no doubt around the country that this bill needed to be passed. After all, Texas wasn't alone. Across the South, there had been violent attempts to interfere with the democratic process.

In 1871, the leading Black citizens of Meridian, Mississippi, were slaughtered for defending democracy—and in 1873, as many as 150 Black men were killed in the Colfax massacre following a contested Louisiana gubernatorial election. The following year, in Alabama, the killing of two Sumter County Republican leaders, one Black and one white, set the stage for a mob to murder seven Black citizens.

In this way, the violent election fraud in Washington County in 1886 was not an outlier, but part of a systematic effort to steal power and subvert the Constitution throughout the South.

And yet, the Republicans in Congress were ultimately unable to maintain their unity in the face of a filibuster challenge. At the time, this was blamed on infighting about short-term political priorities and a need to focus on the economy after the Panic of 1873. But it's also clear that while the moral urgency was there, the political will was not. (Sound familiar?)

How else can you explain failing to move forward when the threat to democracy was so clear?

In the end, the filibuster organized by Senator Coke, an ally and friend of Lafayette Kirk (ringleader of the Washington County vote theft), won out—bringing down the last, best chance for voting rights in Texas and the rest of the South for generations.

"Let the people of each State alone," he said to his colleagues in the Senate. "Let the men control who know each other, the men who are peers, the men who are raised together, the men who are neighbors; let them settle it. Just let us alone; just let the negroes take care of themselves . . . and those whom God has in His Creation . . . decreed by the structure and organization of their brain . . . rule."

The bill was never even voted on in the Senate. It didn't help that President Harrison, who, again, had campaigned on a platform of restoring voting rights, remained on the sidelines for much of the action. It looked like Harrison, along with some of the Senate Republicans, was more interested in solidifying alliances with Southern politicians than in justice for all citizens of the South.

The legislation was dead, as was any hope for federal protection of voting rights in Texas or anywhere else. And, not for the last time, justice for the people of Texas was a casualty of self-serving political expediency in Washington, D.C. Harrison's inaction looks cowardly in the light of history. But if anything, it should remind us that we can't rely on federal action—from distant and insulated U.S. senators and presidential administrations consumed by the calculations leading up to the next midterm election—to guarantee our rights.

In the subsequent decades, Black Americans and other communities of color would be systematically disenfranchised. As a result, they were denied the ability to fully participate in the affairs of their country, to affect the outcome of elections, to hold public office, to engage in civil society and the economy, and to participate in a system of justice that would treat them equally under the law.

But through it all, Black Americans, including in Texas, built a movement that would come closer than at any other time in our history to producing a government of, by, and for the people—all of the people. Their courage and persistence ensured that, seventy-nine years after the Texas Election Outrage, America finally began to look like a democracy.

They didn't wait for the cavalry to come to the rescue. *They* were the cavalry.

———

If the squandered opportunity to extend and protect the franchise in 1890 was born of outrage that originated in Texas, then the successful one of 1965 was born of organizing that ultimately convinced the first Texan president that the right to vote was paramount.

When we think about what we're up against today, it's worth remembering that the challenges that voting rights advocates faced prior to 1965 were much greater. And yet they ultimately overcame them, demonstrating that victory isn't just possible. It's been won before against much bigger odds.

They show us that turning outrage into action is the key.

A little more than twenty years after the failure of the Federal Elections Bill in 1890, Ida B. Wells—the trailblazing journalist and activist—founded the Alpha Suffrage Club to advocate for the full enfranchisement of all Americans, including all Black Americans. She understood that the traditional bastions of political power were insufficient to the task of overcoming suppression. What was needed was a "new power, [a] new molder of public sentiment, to accomplish the reforms that the pulpit and the law have failed to do." She also firmly believed that if democracy were to be fully realized in America, Black women must be at the vanguard.

Later, in the 1950s, Septima Clark's "Citizenship Schools" taught reading and civics to Southern Black Americans interested in registering to vote, helping them withstand the indignity of the literacy and civics tests imposed by county registrars intent upon denying them the franchise. By 1961, she was supervising seven hundred instructors who were responsible for forty-two thousand new Black voters. The Southern Christian Leadership Conference (SCLC) adopted the schools and Clark was asked to run them on a much larger scale. Between 1961 and 1969, seven hundred thousand African Americans in the South were registered to vote.

Bob Moses followed Clark's lead in Mississippi, personally escorting those he had trained for the literacy and civics tests to register in a state where less than 7 percent of eligible African Americans had been able to do so. Beaten and jailed for the courage of his convictions, Moses provided the example of sacrifice that the fight would require if it were to be successful.

———

Wells, Clark, and Moses are but three of thousands who were willing, at extraordinary risk and sacrifice, to provide the leadership on civil

11

and voting rights that was missing from the chambers of Congress and the halls of justice at the end of the nineteenth century and the beginning of the twentieth.

Without federal protection—in fact, with the federal government having completely abdicated its role to uphold the Constitution— they persisted in working to gain the franchise for those who'd been targeted by the most violent and systemic forms of suppression.

They did not know when, or even if, their efforts would produce the democracy for which they fought. They had no expectation that those in the highest offices would help them share in political power. They just knew that no one else would do this for them, and that they would have to keep fighting, working, and sacrificing until their government did the right thing.

———

After the Civil Rights Bill of 1964 had become law, abolishing seg- regation across all fifty states, Martin Luther King Jr. pushed Pres- ident Lyndon Johnson to make voting rights his next priority. He visited the White House, alongside SCLC executive director An- drew Young, and told the president why he should act to save our democracy.

Wary of imposing another heavy lift on Congress following the toll of passing the Civil Rights Act, Johnson told them that though he understood the importance of federal voting rights, he didn't "have the power" to move Congress. Young later recalled that as King left the meeting, he turned to him and said, "We've got to get this pres- ident some power."

Unlike in 1890, this time it would not be left to faraway senators to decide the outcome of the most important question of American democracy. It would be up to the people with the most to gain or lose. And Dr. King, along with other leaders of the civil rights movement, decided to take the fight to the streets of Selma, Alabama, where most of the citizens were Black but hardly any had been able to register to vote.

As it turned out, the protests in Selma ended up being the single greatest generator of political power—both for the movement for voting rights and for President Johnson's effort to compel Congress to take action that year—that the civil rights movement had seen.

After "Bloody Sunday," when John Lewis was beaten nearly to death as he led a march for voting rights across the Edmund Pettus Bridge and images of the violence unleashed on him and his fellow marchers were beamed out of television screens across the nation, President Johnson convened a joint session of Congress to implore them to pass the Voting Rights Act.

He finally had the power he needed.

"At times, history and fate meet at a single time in a single place to shape a turning point in man's unending search for freedom," Johnson began, seeking to place Selma within the proud tradition of sacrifice and struggle that had gained American liberty.

So it was at Lexington and Concord. So it was a century ago at Appomattox. So it was last week in Selma, Alabama.

There, long-suffering men and women peacefully protested the denial of their rights as Americans. Many were brutally assaulted. One good man—a man of God—was killed.

There is no cause for pride in what has happened in Selma.

There is no cause for self-satisfaction in the long denial of equal rights of millions of Americans. But there is cause for hope and for faith in our democracy in what is happening here tonight.

The hope that the president spoke of was that Congress would finally pass voting rights.

"We have already waited a hundred years and more, and the time for waiting is gone," Johnson continued.

No matter how violent, insidious, or creative the effort to deny the vote, the president called on Congress to extend and protect full citizenship to all American citizens.

This bill will strike down restrictions to voting in *all* elections—federal, state, and local—which have been used to deny Negroes the right to vote.

It will establish a simple, uniform standard which cannot be used, however ingenious the effort, to flout our Constitution.

It will provide for citizens to be registered by officials of the United States Government if the state officials refuse to register them.

It will eliminate tedious, unnecessary lawsuits which delay the right to vote.

Finally, this legislation will insure that properly registered individuals are not prohibited from voting.

I will welcome the suggestions from all the members of Congress—I have no doubt that I will get some—on ways and means to strengthen this law and to make it effective.

But experience has plainly shown that this is the only path to carry out the command of the Constitution. To those who seek to avoid action by their national Government in their home communities, who want to and who seek to maintain purely local control over elections, the answer is simple: Open your polling places to all your people.

Allow men and women to register and vote whatever the color of their skin.

Extend the rights of citizenship to every citizen of this land.

The next day, King wrote to Johnson from Selma. "Your speech to the joint session of Congress last night was the most moving eloquent unequivocal and passionate plea for human rights ever made by any president of this nation. You evidenced amazing understanding of the depth and dimensions of the problems that we face in our struggle, your tone was sincere throughout and your persuasive power never more forceful."

The power of a vigorous and unbending activism met the willingness of a president to exercise the full power of his office. The bill passed both houses of Congress and was signed into law on the sixth of August of that year.

Through the Voting Rights Act of 1965, America began to systematically address access to the ballot box and work to end both violent and nonviolent forms of voter intimidation—making sure states would no longer be "left alone" to determine which Americans would be allowed to vote.

———

No longer could poll taxes, literacy tests, or recitations of state constitutions be required in order to deter or prevent Americans from registering to vote or casting a ballot. A much bigger electorate, much more reflective of the country at large, would decide the outcome of local, state, and federal elections.

The Voting Rights Act also meant that the Americans who could stand for and win elected office would be much more diverse than they had ever been, at least since Reconstruction. And while some states would continue to try to subvert the letter and spirit of the law, they were met by a federal Department of Justice that, by and large, was able to stop efforts to disenfranchise voters through identification requirements, polling location closures, or racially gerrymandered districts.

That is, until the *Shelby* ruling in 2013, which abolished a requirement to "preclear" changes states made to their voting laws with the Department of Justice. Over the next few years, Southern states began adopting laws that flew in the face of what the VRA had protected for the previous fifty years. And Texas was at the front of that pack, its new laws limiting opportunities to vote and participate in the multiracial democracy that our state helped to create in 1965.

And now, what once might have been seen as a momentary slip into something less than full democracy has clearly become a slide toward something else altogether: authoritarian government won through intimidation and violence instead of votes.

On January 6, 2021, a violent, organized plot to overturn a lawfully decided election was set in motion by President Donald Trump and a number of white supremacist organizations. Like the People's Party partisans in 1886, many arrived at the Capitol masked, disguised, and armed. And like the Washington County ballot thieves, they attempted through violence and terror to steal the votes of a lawfully, legitimately decided election.

Though the 2021 attack on the Capitol was unsuccessful in the short term and Congress certified the election of Joe Biden as the forty-sixth president of the United States, the larger and longer effort to roll back the right to vote and undermine free and fair elections in this country has been extraordinarily effective.

In the months following the insurrection, the violence at the Capitol was succeeded by a coordinated attempt to rewrite election laws—making it harder for voters of color, among others, to register or cast a ballot. These efforts have become law in fourteen states, including ones where election margins are often thin, like Georgia, Florida, Iowa, and Texas. It's not unlike the organized legislative effort following the failure of the federal government in 1890 to respond to the Texas Outrage that disenfranchised Black voters and other voters of color throughout the South for more than seven decades.

But that failure can serve as a warning for us today. Understanding our past means that it doesn't have to be our future.

After the defeat of federal voting rights legislation at the end of the nineteenth century, Texas lost its democracy, at least for the next several generations. And in the absence of voting rights, every manner of Jim Crow repression took form, from poll taxes to literacy tests to mandatory annual reregistration of the voter rolls.

And the informal "whites-only primary"—once the work of disparate groups like the People's Party—would, by 1923, become an official state law of Texas, eliminating Black Americans from our state's elections entirely.

But while Texas has proven throughout its history to be one of the centers of voter suppression, we have also demonstrated that we can produce the champions who can overcome these laws and unlock democracy not only for Texas, but for the country as a whole.

That is the fight organizers, volunteers, and everyday citizens across our state are waging once again. They're marching, testifying at public hearings, knocking on doors, registering their fellow Texans to vote. They're putting in the work to ensure that our future will be more democratic than our past.

———

I've been asked: Given all the other pressing challenges that we face, why should we be fighting for the right to vote?

If this were only theoretical or academic, I'd understand the need to prioritize other issues. However, every other issue imaginable—from our ability to see a doctor, to the quality of our kids' schools, to the kind of job we can get, to the expectation to be treated and judged fairly within our criminal justice system—is dependent on the right to vote. If your voice is not heard, if your vote is not counted, if your community is not represented, then you will, at a minimum, be less likely to realize the opportunities that this country makes possible; at worst, you will be targeted for and unprotected from some of its most violent abuses.

If we accept that democracy is foundational to our mutual *and* individual success, then it's on all of us to save it, restore it, and expand it until every eligible citizen is fully included. We all benefit from democracy when everyone is able to participate in our democracy. Everyone's in or it doesn't work.

The question, then, is, what do we do now?

There's the negative example, of what not to do. That's 1890, when those in power acknowledged that our democracy was in jeopardy without doing anything to save it. And, so far, that could describe those in power in 2022. Despite controlling the White House, the Senate, and the House of Representatives, Democrats have been unable to pass legislation combating the attacks on elections taking place across the country.

But the fight for the right to vote isn't over—not until we say it is. And this time, we must ensure that it doesn't take Congress another seventy-nine years to do the right thing.

That means taking inspiration from voting rights leaders who came before us, the generations of activists who inherited an even less inclusive democracy—one where many were killed for so much as trying to vote—but did not let that stop them from fighting to build a better one.

I've come to realize through the aid of history how fortunate we are, at this moment, to be the heirs to this struggle, this service, and this sacrifice. This democracy—as imperfect as it may be—is what sets us apart, not only from so much of the rest of the planet but from so much of human history. We are truly exceptional in that sense. And not for any reason other than that those who preceded us made it possible. Those who wrote and adopted our foundational documents, which defined our aspirations even if the founders themselves did not live up to them; those who fought in wars of independence, of emancipation, and of freedom, and willingly gave their lives for our ability to freely decide our future; those who took a stand against oppression and segregation in our own country, risking and too often losing their lives in the process, so that more Americans could realize the promise laid out in those foundational documents; they are the ones we have to thank for what is possible today.

In other words, while it can be tempting to succumb to despair, given the perilous state of our democracy, we should remember that we are the heirs to something extraordinary, made possible only through generations of significant sacrifice. And we have the exceptional fortune of being the generation that has the chance to save it.

What we do with this inheritance—this democracy that so many gave their lives for—will define us, and by extension, this country for the generations to come. We don't want the people of the future—our kids and grandkids and their kids and grandkids—to look back on us and condemn us for squandering the legacy established over the last 246 years.

To put it as positively as I can, there is no better time to be alive if you love this country and care about our form of government. It's never been under greater attack in our lifetimes—and not since 1965 has there been a better opportunity to fight for it.

That's what draws me to the work that I do. Running for and serving in public office, volunteering for other candidates, testifying at public hearings on elections bills, helping to register voters across Texas, speaking out about the challenges to our democracy, and joining my fellow Americans to do the work to save it—like so many others, I'm trying to do my part, to live up to those who've faced much longer and tougher odds and kept trying nonetheless.

Those champions of democracy are my heroes, champions like Lawrence Nixon—a loving father and husband, a doctor, a pillar of his community, a civil rights trailblazer, a proud Texan, and a man who forced this country to move closer to its founding ideal.

Though Nixon's father had been enslaved at birth, and Nixon himself had grown up in a time of violent segregation, he would rise to meet one of the great challenges of American democracy. And he would do it from the border city of El Paso, Texas.

PART I

PART

I

"I've Got to Try"

W hen Dr. Lawrence Aaron Nixon walked into the fire
station to cast his ballot in the Democratic primary, he
knew full well what he was up against.

After all, this was July 1924—and he was a Black man in Texas,
a state where people who looked like him were not supposed to be
able to vote.

The year before, free from any federal voting rights protections
thanks to the defeat of the 1890 Federal Elections Bill, the Texas
legislature had passed Senate Bill 44, which read:

> In no event shall a negro be eligible to participate in a Dem-
> ocratic primary election held in the State of Texas, and should a
> negro vote in a Democratic primary election, such ballot shall be

23

void, and election officials are herein directed to throw out such a ballot and not count the same.

During this time, and through most of the twentieth century, the Democratic primary was the only meaningful election in the state. Nominally, a Republican Party in Texas had existed, but it was so anemic that it could barely function. This meant that Texas was essentially a single-party state under control of the Democrats, so if you were prevented from voting in the party's primary—as was now the case for every Black Texan—you had no say in who would represent you in government.

The "white primary law" was intended to codify in statute what had been practiced informally across much of the state for the last three decades: whites would control political power in Texas.

El Paso, where Nixon lived, was not free of the kind of discrimination that led to these practices. For decades, Black El Pasoans had been limited in where they could live, where they could sit on streetcars or in movie theaters, and where they could receive services. ("I Don't Work for Negroes," wrote one dentist advertising in the *El Paso Herald*.)

Still, compared to much of the rest of Texas—especially Marshall, where Nixon had grown up—El Paso had historically been much more welcoming of Black Americans.

That relative tolerance might have been what attracted Dr. Nixon to the border town in the first place.

After growing up in deep East Texas and living briefly in the central part of the state, he packed up his belongings, boarded a train, and made his way to West Texas in 1910.

But the El Paso that greeted Lawrence Nixon when he arrived

at the Union Depot in January of that year was completely different from the El Paso he'd briefly visited as a child, then a small outpost at the edge of Texas. Twenty years later, it was a thriving, growing community, a place that was essential to anyone doing anything of any significance in the American Southwest.

———

The train station itself was a celebrated local landmark. Completed four years before Nixon's arrival, it was designed by Chicago architect Daniel Burnham in neoclassical style. Sunlight poured through the high Diocletian windows onto a pristine marble floor and lit up the symmetrical pillars and detailed architectural ornaments that would have made a third-century Roman citizen as proud as it did the El Pasoans of the twentieth. A Harvey House restaurant served fresh seafood and raw oysters delivered by rail from the coasts. It was clear that El Paso considered itself a leading American city and was taking the steps necessary to realize that ambition.

It was no accident that the city fathers chose Burnham to design this prominent landmark in the tradition of great public spaces that recalled the height of the Roman Empire. "Make no little plans," Burnham had said. "They have no magic to stir men's blood and probably themselves will not be realized."

Burnham's counsel was the prevailing wisdom of the day: dream big enough and anything is possible.

The year before Nixon's arrival, President William Howard Taft had arrived at the same Union Depot to meet with his Mexican counterpart, Porfirio Díaz, at the El Paso Chamber of Commerce, the first-ever summit between leaders from the two countries. Though Chihuahua governor Enrique Creel officially served as the meeting's interpreter, the two presidents were able to speak each other's native tongue well enough to understand the other. All went remarkably well until President Taft's chair collapsed under his weight at the end of the meeting.

Within a year of the first U.S.-Mexico summit, a prosperous Mexican landowner named Francisco Madero would challenge Díaz in that country's national election. Defeated in what turned out to be a heavily rigged contest, and jailed for good measure, Madero escaped Mexico and came to El Paso, setting up the provisional headquarters of the Mexican revolutionary forces only blocks away from the Union Depot.

Within months, he would defeat Díaz's government army in the battle for Ciudad Juárez, and by 1911, he was sitting in the president's chair in Mexico City.

In this way, El Paso had already borne witness to one revolution against a rigged democracy by the time Nixon had moved there—and the ground was fertile for another one.

———

As the only all-weather pass through the Rocky Mountains, the biggest U.S. city on the border with Mexico, and the center of commerce in the greater Southwest, El Paso played an outsized role in the American West.

Two years after his visit to El Paso, and only months after the Battle of Juárez, President Taft signed legislation that would make the territories of New Mexico and Arizona the next two states admitted to the Union. The plan was to hold an initial statehood convention and celebratory jubilee for the two new states, but there was no city in either territory large enough to host these events. So a competition was launched among the significant cities of the West for the honor, with El Paso ultimately beating out Los Angeles.

In October 1911, the city hosted the new governors of Arizona and New Mexico, as well as the governors of Texas, Chihuahua, and Sonora, for a weeklong celebration, the likes of which had never been seen in the western states. The members of the various delegations whooped it up in an unending series of banquets, parades, dances, and balls. A baseball tournament between the five states was held, with El Paso fielding its own team. In a sign of how seriously they took the competition, El Paso recruited Chick Brandom, who had helped the Pittsburgh Pirates win the World Series in 1908, to pitch for their side.

This was the kind of enterprising, creative, and proudly binational city that Lawrence Nixon stepped into when he stepped off that train in January 1910. It couldn't have been more different from his hometown of Marshall or the other Southern cities in which he'd lived. It was aspirational, wildly ambitious, and brand-new. It wasn't yet set or defined. The lines between countries and cultures blurred. Opportunity abounded, and not only for white men.

That marked a stark contrast from the city Nixon had previously called home: Cameron, Texas. Located in East-Central Texas between Austin and Waco, Cameron had been a shot in the dark for Nixon, who was encouraged to move there sight unseen by a good friend after Nixon graduated from medical school in 1906. He soon despaired of his decision, writing that he had "never before seen [Black] people living in such wretched surroundings."

His misgivings were confirmed the next year when he witnessed the lynching of Alex Johnson, a Black man accused of attacking a white girl. More than five hundred people showed up to witness the hanging, and though Nixon was safely behind the doors of his medical office, he could still hear Johnson's cries. There would be another lynching of a Black man, Coke Mills, a little more than a dozen miles outside of Cameron in 1909, just weeks before Nixon left for El Paso.

El Paso was a new, growing city firmly focused on the future. It was oriented toward the West, not the South, and it was closer to the state capitals of Arizona, New Mexico, Sonora, and Chihuahua than it was to Austin. It was as far away from Marshall and Cameron and other Texas redoubts of Confederate resentment as you could get without leaving the state.

It also had Ciudad Juárez, across the river, where Black Americans had more rights than in their home country.

As Langston Hughes wrote when he visited the two communities in the 1930s, "It was strange to find that just by stepping across an invisible line into Mexico, a Negro could buy a beer in any bar, sit anywhere in the movies, or eat in any restaurant, so suddenly did Jim Crow disappear, and Americans visiting Juárez, who would not drink beside a Negro in Texas, did so in Mexico."

If the twin sister cities of El Paso and Ciudad Juárez—united, not divided, by the Rio Grande—were about new beginnings, new starts, new creation, then Nixon was going to take full advantage of it. Confirming that he was finally in the right place, Nixon sent for his young wife, Esther, and their one-year-old son, Lawrence Joseph, to join him in El Paso. He set up his medical practice and quickly became engaged in the civic life of the community.

He helped organize a Methodist congregation, voted in the Democratic primary and the November general election, and in 1913, he joined other Black El Pasoans in creating the El Paso Lyceum and Civic Improvement Association. After petitioning the NAACP to charter a branch in El Paso, by the summer of 1914, the El Paso Lyceum became the first NAACP chapter in the state.

Nixon was elected as the new organization's first executive committee chairman and helped focus the group's efforts on Jim Crow practices that circumscribed life for the African American community and produced daily humiliations, like the time Nixon and his son were booted from their seats at the circus for sitting too close to the show and ushered into the far back of the tent with the other Black patrons.

Though denied equal treatment under the law and faced with the indignity of Jim Crow, Nixon had found a home in El Paso. The challenges of discrimination produced a drive for action and justice within him that might have been fatal in other parts of the state, certainly in Marshall and Cameron.

He also fell in love with a culture that was different from anything he'd yet experienced. Setting up his residence and practice in the Mexican American immigrant neighborhood of Segundo Barrio, Nixon quickly learned Spanish and saw primarily Black and Mexican American patients.

Segundo Barrio was at that time, as it still is today, a neighborhood of immigrants from Mexico and Latin America. Some refer to it as "The Ellis Island of the Americas," in part because so many American families can trace their roots back to this historic neighborhood that has two international bridges connecting it to Ciudad Juárez. Those who lived in Segundo Barrio when the Nixon family arrived would have largely been the lowest-wage laborers and craftsmen, who with their families lived in sprawling tenements not subject to traditional city code enforcement, like the Seis Infiernos (or "Six Hells") tenements on South Ochoa Street.

But Segundo Barrio was also home to artists, educators, doctors, revolutionaries, poets, and historians. Mariano Azuelo wrote the story of Mexican revolutionaries in a series of pamphlets inserted into the *El Paso del Norte* newspaper in an apartment just blocks from Nixon's medical office. Those inserts were later collected and published as *Los de abajo* (sometimes translated into English as *The Underdogs*), which became *the* novel of the Mexican Revolution.

And as much as it was defined by the Mexican immigrant experience, Segundo Barrio was also home to a number of African Americans, including the Nixon family, especially since Jim Crow limited the neighborhoods where they could live. Henry Flipper, who had been born enslaved and rose to become the first African American graduate of West Point, called the corner of Third and Oregon in Segundo Barrio home for a while.

In other words, Segundo Barrio (literally, "Second Ward") was a neighborhood of people who, though limited by custom and law to second-class status in the wider city despite their talent, accomplishments, and potential, were nevertheless able to contribute to the success of the community and the country.

But its second-class status meant that it also received the scarcest of resources and the least amount of positive government attention, and bore the brunt of the toughest challenges facing the city as a whole. When the global flu pandemic of 1918 came to El Paso, it hit Segundo Barrio especially hard, taking Nixon's wife the following year, but sparing his young son. As was the practice at the time, family members cared for his child. Now alone, and grieving, Nixon poured his energies into political action, before eventually remarrying, to a fellow activist named Drusilla Tandy Porter.

Together, according to Will Guzmán, who wrote the definitive biography of Nixon, Lawrence and Drusilla would spend decades "building organizations for various social justice causes including access to the ballot, eliminating the poll tax, exposing structural racism, and challenging Jane and Jim Crow."

They would eventually move closer to the all-Black Douglass School, in the nearby Magoffin neighborhood. But the community of underdogs and immigrants in Segundo Barrio who first welcomed Dr. Nixon would undoubtedly influence him for the remainder of his life.

In his new practice at the corner of Willow and Myrtle—in a neighborhood of mixed industrial, retail, and residential buildings— Nixon further rose as a community leader. Whether it was serving in his church, leading the NAACP, or working with the city government to construct a swimming pool for Black children, Nixon embraced the opportunity to serve. Along with practicing medicine and caring for his patients, civic engagement became central to his purpose in life.

And so it must have come as a rude shock to him following the adoption of the white primary law by the Texas legislature in 1923 that, after more than a decade of dedication to the public life of this burgeoning, ambitious community, he would no longer be able to vote in Texas elections.

As if unable to accept this injustice and too set in his path of civic involvement, Nixon still paid his annual poll tax in January 1924. He also continued to negotiate with El Paso's newly elected mayor on the funding and location for the public swimming pool that would serve Black El Pasoans. And he voted in the May bond election that year to help ensure its passage. (This was only possible because it was a municipal, nonpartisan race, and therefore wasn't subject to the white primary law.)

Meanwhile, unbeknownst to Nixon, William Pickens, the national field secretary, was looking for someone to challenge the new Texas voting law in court. While other states had worked to prevent African Americans from voting, none but Texas had taken the extreme measure of enshrining the prohibition in statute.

The ideal candidate for the suit had to meet a narrow set of conditions: they had to be a Black voter who had paid their poll tax; they had to be a consistently registered Democrat; and, most important, as Pickens put it, "we are looking for someone who is not afraid."

Of all the possible Black voters in Texas, he chose Nixon, who fit the bill as perfectly as could have been hoped.

Nixon readily accepted the challenge to become the lead plaintiff in fighting the white primary law, perhaps not knowing the difficulty and duration of the battle before him.

And so, on the morning of July 26, 1924, Nixon walked the three blocks to his normal polling location, Fire Station No. 5 on Texas Avenue, to try to vote in the Democratic primary. There, he was greeted by the election judges, Champ Herndon and Charles Porras, both of whom he would have called his friends.

They made polite small talk, asking about each other's health. This must have been a familiar routine, given the number of elections in which Nixon had voted at this same location.

And then Nixon displayed his poll tax receipt in order to vote. The tone of the conversation changed, and one of the judges painfully told him, "Dr. Nixon, you know we can't let you vote."

"I know you can't," he answered. "But I've got to try."

2

This Time, They Voted

I t was the first step in a journey that would take Nixon to the Supreme Court and ultimately break the white primary.

The right person in the right place had met the right moment. The same state whose antidemocratic election outrages had provoked Congress to try to take up voter protection legislation in 1890; the state whose senator had filibustered that effort to death the following year; the state that, uniquely, had enshrined whites-only voting in statute—that state had produced a man committed to bringing about a true multiracial democracy.

But while Dr. Nixon may have known this fight would require extraordinary courage and persistence, it's hard to imagine that he knew he'd be waging it for the next twenty years.

It started on July 31, 1924, when the NAACP hired Nixon's own attorney, Fred Knollenberg, to file suit on his behalf in the federal district court in El Paso. Knollenberg argued that Nixon's constitutional rights under the Fifteenth Amendment ("The right of citizens of the United States to vote shall not be denied or abridged by the United States or by any State on account of race, color, or previous condition of servitude") had been violated; and that being denied the right to vote in the Democratic primary in Texas was tantamount to being stripped of this basic right of citizenship, since the results of the Democratic primary were definitive for nearly all election outcomes in the state.

The opposing attorneys argued that the primary election was not really an election after all, but a "purely political matter" best left to the purview of the political parties.

The judge bought that argument and dismissed the suit without explanation.

Having anticipated this outcome, Nixon and Knollenberg appealed directly to the Supreme Court of the United States to reverse the dismissal, bypassing the U.S. Court of Appeals. It was a gamble, but it worked, and the Supreme Court set the case for the October term in 1926.

In the meantime, there would be another state election with whites-only primary laws. So, in July 1926, Nixon once again walked the three blocks from his office to Fire Station No. 5. He once again tried to vote. And he once again was turned back because of the color of his skin.

Nixon's case was finally called for argument in January 1927. Knollenberg answered questions from Justice Oliver Wendell Holmes Jr. and the other members of the court. Though he felt that Holmes was sympathetic, he worried that the adversarial nature of the questions asked by others might lead to a majority opinion against Nixon. The State of Texas, through Governor-elect Dan Moody and the attorney general, submitted a brief in defense of the white primary law, again arguing that the primary was not an election. But this time, the justices seemed to see right through that argument.

On March 7, the decision was announced: the Supreme Court unanimously decided in favor of Dr. Nixon in *Nixon v. Herndon*. Justice Holmes wrote the opinion, one that focused on equal rights and the Fourteenth Amendment instead of voting rights and the Fifteenth Amendment.

"We find it unnecessary to consider the Fifteenth Amendment," Holmes wrote, "because it seems to us hard to imagine a more direct and obvious infringement of the Fourteenth." He went on to write, "The statute of Texas . . . assumes to forbid negroes to take part in a primary election . . . discriminating against them by the distinction of color alone."

While the victory was celebrated by Nixon and his supporters (the *El Paso Herald* called it "the most significant case ever carried to the Supreme Court of the United States by an El Paso attorney"), and while the court's decision unequivocally declared the Texas voting law unconstitutional, a significant problem remained: the focus on equal protection instead of the right to vote had left the Texas legislature a lot of room to maneuver—and that's exactly what it did.

It's worth noting that it was not only the most ardent white supremacists and openly racist members of the legislature who wanted to stop Black Texans from voting. Sure, there were outwardly racist representatives like A. R. Stout of Ellis County, who said things like, "I had rather take my chances on handling the 'n———,'" but there were also folks like Dan Moody, the "reformer" governor, who cloaked the same racism and hostility to African Americans in far more carefully worded language.

At the time, Governor Moody was known as a young, bold leader in Texas politics who had fought the Klan at the height of its power in the 1920s, prosecuted corruption in the highest positions of public trust, and decisively defeated the dominant Ferguson machine (which had previously elected both "Pa" and "Ma" Ferguson governor). But despite that reputation, Governor Moody would go on to circumvent the Supreme Court decision and guarantee continued Black disenfranchisement.

He called an emergency special session of the state legislature to repeal the white primary law and replace it with a measure that would allow "the executive committee of the several political parties to determine the qualifications requisite to membership in such parties."

In other words: if the Supreme Court says it's unconstitutional for the state legislature to decide whether Black Texans can vote in the Democratic primary, we'll allow the party itself, through its executive committee, to do it.

The bill passed. The white primary law gave the Texas Democratic Party's executive committee the ability to bar Black voters, ensuring that Nixon and every other Black Texan would be prevented from voting in the 1928 election that would determine their governor, senator, U.S. representative, state representative, county commissioner, and a host of other local offices—not to mention to whom Texas would pledge its electoral college votes for president. And because there was literally no Republican primary in Texas (the GOP having polled less than the requisite number of votes in the previous election to trigger one), Black Texans were completely disenfranchised.

Nonetheless, on July 28 of that year, Dr. Nixon yet again walked the three blocks from his office on Myrtle to Fire Station No. 5 on Texas Avenue. He waited in line with the other voters and, once at the front of the line, presented his poll tax receipt. The election judges once again told him he would not be able to vote.

And in March of the next year, after negotiating with the NAACP's legal team on strategy as well as payment for Knollenberg's work, Nixon and Knollenberg once again filed suit in the federal district court in El Paso.

The district court judge found for the defendants in this case, the two new election judges who had denied Nixon the right to vote, asserting essentially that a primary is not an election and that the Democratic Party is a voluntary organization that is legally allowed to deny membership to anyone for any reason.

Nixon and Knollenberg appealed. The case, *Nixon v. Condon*, was sent to the circuit court of appeals in Fort Worth, set for November 1930. That meant that yet another Texas election would pass without Nixon or any Black Texan being able to vote. And then, in the spring of 1931, they received even worse news: the district court's decision was affirmed, with the circuit court writing that "a political party is a voluntary association, and as such has the inherent power to prescribe the qualifications of its members."

Nixon appealed once again to the Supreme Court, arguing that it was clearly the state of Texas, and not only the Democratic Party, that sought to deny Black Texans the right to vote. After all, he reasoned, why else would the statute delegating the authority to the parties' executive committees be declared an emergency? It was only an emergency for the legislature, because the Supreme Court's 1927 decision striking down the white primary law would mean Black Texans would be able to vote in the next primary election—something the legislature was determined to stop.

And furthermore, could anyone say, with a straight face, that the state of Texas was not in charge of primary elections? The supporting brief written by Knollenberg made the case:

> The time, place, and manner of holding Primary Elections, as well as of determining and contesting the results thereof, are comprehensively and minutely described by statutory provisions. Having already assumed control over primary elections, it proceeded by Chapter 67 of the laws of 1927 to delegate to the state executive committee of every political party in the state the power to prescribe qualifications for membership and who should be qualified to vote or otherwise participate in the political parties.

The Supreme Court accepted the case for review in October 1931, and on May 2, 1932, Justice Benjamin Cardozo, who had replaced Justice Oliver Wendell Holmes on the court, delivered the opinion of the five-to-four majority in favor of the plaintiffs. It began by noting that this was not the first time that Dr. Nixon "found it necessary to invoke the jurisdiction of the federal courts in vindication of privileges secured to him by the federal Constitution."

And while the ruling made clear that the Texas legislature had discriminated "invidiously between white citizens and black," and once again invoked the Fourteenth Amendment to justify the court's responsibility to "level . . . these barriers of color," the decision in Nixon's favor did not address whether the Democratic Party's barring of Black voters was unconstitutional. Instead, the justices decided on the much narrower issue of whether the state of Texas could recognize the authority of the party's executive committee to disenfranchise Black voters. The court said it could not. But it refused to rule on whether the party as a whole might be able to do the same.

"As to that," Cardozo wrote, "decision must be postponed until decision becomes necessary."

The case was referred back to the district court in El Paso and was heard in October 1932 on the basis of the Supreme Court's ruling. Ultimately, the decision confirmed that Nixon "was deprived of his right to vote in the Democratic Primary," and awarded him the symbolic damages of one dollar.

It was Nixon's second Supreme Court victory, again won with the help of Knollenberg and the NAACP. In the meantime, yet another statewide election had taken place and Nixon, as well as every other Black Texan, was once again prohibited from participating in it. And because the Cardozo decision had ruled narrowly on whether the state could recognize the power of the Democratic Party Executive Committee to bar Black citizens from voting, rather than on the larger issue of whether any party primary could exclude them, Nixon knew that the fight was far from over.

In fact, not even a month after the Supreme Court's decision in *Nixon v. Condon*, the state Democratic convention passed a resolution that read: "Be it resolved that all white citizens of the State of Texas who are qualified to vote under the constitution and laws of the State shall be eligible to membership in the Democratic party, and, as such, to participate in its deliberations."

This had to have been a particularly tough time for Nixon. By the next statewide election, in 1934, it had been ten years since he first told the election judges in El Paso that though they said he could not vote, he would still try. And it would be another ten years until he finally could.

———

In July 1934, another Black voter filed a new voting rights challenge, this time in Houston. The case of *Grovey v. Townsend* made it to the Supreme Court only to be struck down, as the court by this time was far more reactionary than the one that had decided *Herndon* and *Condon*. Its unanimous ruling claimed that the Democratic Party had not denied Black voters "any rights guaranteed by the Fourteenth and Fifteenth Amendments."

Nevertheless, Nixon kept paying his poll tax every year. Perhaps he did so on the chance that the courts or the legislature would provide some reprieve from the indignity under which he labored. Perhaps it was merely a demonstration of his faith in democracy—or even a stubborn assertion that he had the right to vote and would continue to do his part even if those who represented him in public office wouldn't do theirs. El Paso radio stations took to calling him as the biannual primary elections approached to ask him if he was going to vote. He responded the same way, every time: "I'm going to try."

As the Texas government and the state Democratic Party dug in on all-white voting, they also began to define other groups of Texans as "nonwhite." For example, in 1934, Mexican Americans in Travis County, home to the state capital in Austin, were prevented from casting their ballots. The local Democratic Party had taken the position that they did not belong to the "white" race.

In 1936, the El Paso city registrar followed suit and announced that Mexican Americans would no longer be considered "white" and would henceforth be registered as "colored" on the city rolls. This meant that Latinos would join Black El Pasoans in being denied the right to vote. Ironically, that would include Charles Porras, one of the two election judges who had told Nixon that he couldn't vote in that first white primary in 1924.

As the years wore on, Nixon must have wondered whether the effort was worth the cost. I can imagine his family and friends encouraging him to "move on," since, despite two signal Supreme Court victories, he had still not won the right to vote. Were the radio stations and newspapers mocking him by asking him if he was going to attempt to vote again? Or were they giving him a chance to broadcast the courage of his convictions and inspire others to have hope and act on it—as he had?

Whatever private concerns he may have had, he still pushed on—paying his poll tax, engaging with reporters, and leading the various civic organizations he had helped to establish over the years.

In 1940, another front in the fight opened in Houston, designed to take advantage of the fact that seven of the nine justices who'd decided *Grovey* had resigned or died, and had since been replaced by President Franklin Roosevelt's more liberal nominees.

Lonnie Smith—like Nixon, a doctor, an officer in his local NAACP, and a strong civil rights advocate—attempted to vote at his Harris County polling place in June 1940, presented his poll tax receipt, and was refused by the election judges on duty. Like Nixon, Smith took the case first to the federal district court. After it was dismissed, Smith appealed to the U.S. circuit court and in this trial was represented by the chief legal officer for the NAACP's Legal Defense Fund, Thurgood Marshall. Losing, as expected, before the Fifth Circuit, Marshall was able to get the case before the Supreme Court, with argument set for November 1943. There, Marshall was joined by the dean of the Howard University Law School, William Hastie.

On April 3, 1944, the court decided in favor of Smith, with only one dissenting vote. The majority opinion found that party primaries could not legally discriminate and must allow all citizens "a right to participate in the choice of elected officials without restriction by any state because of race." The justices noted that "constitutional rights would be of little value if they could be thus indirectly denied" by allowing political parties to disenfranchise voters based on race.

Conrey Bryson, author of *Dr. Lawrence A. Nixon and the White Primary*, notes that even though the decision was announced long after the deadline to pay the 1944 poll tax (a requirement to vote in primary elections in Texas), 290 African Americans in El Paso had already paid their $1.75 for the ability to vote that year. Just like Lawrence Nixon, they had faith that democracy and justice would ultimately prevail.

No mention was made in the local papers, or the national press for that matter, of the fact that it was Nixon who had begun this fight and that it was his landmark Supreme Court victories that had paved the way for *Smith v. Allwright*. As I learned from talking with Edna McIver, Lawrence and Drusilla's surviving daughter, that may have been just how he'd wanted it.

Edna told me that her parents never really spoke of this time in their lives, and in fact, the first time she learned of her father's role in securing the right to vote in Texas was in the sixth grade in her segregated all-Black elementary school in El Paso. The teacher asked the class who had filed the critical court challenges to begin the successful reintegration of voting in Texas. Edna raised her hand first, but she didn't have the correct answer. "This is one time, Edna, you do not know the answer?" the teacher scolded.

"I didn't," Edna explained to me. The teacher told her it was her father. "I was shocked. So when I came home for lunch, I asked about that and Momma and Daddy said, 'We didn't want to tell you because we didn't want you to have that burden.'"

Nixon saw his work not as something that distinguished him personally so much as something that was necessary to protect the rights of his fellow Americans. And he knew that this burden fell disproportionately on Black Americans like him. In a letter to the executive secretary of the NAACP years after the *Smith* decision, Nixon wrote, "The negro in El Paso, as in all other localities, means to fight always to preserve the Constitution of the United States and to make democracy a fact in this land, and not a lying cloak to hide behind."

———

As I have become more involved in voting rights work over the years, I continue to turn to Nixon for inspiration, convinced that he is the example we need at this moment.

Nixon did what he knew had to be done, regardless of the cost and consequence to him and regardless of the fact that when he began this fight, he had no idea how it would end. Now that we find ourselves facing the greatest threat to democracy since the crucial battles of the civil rights era, and nowhere more so than in Texas, we must look to the heroes of our past to guide us toward the victories that our country needs.

That's why so many Texans have been fighting for voting rights since the *Shelby* decision—signing up with organizations like Powered by People, MOVE, Black Voters Matter, and the Texas Freedom

Network. Because like those who came before us, we refuse to sit back and allow those in power to destroy our democracy.

It isn't easy to get involved. Why spend the time on something that's so hard to do when there are so many other pressing priorities? Why get your hopes up when, judging from our recent history and our current odds, they're likely to get crushed in the end?

These are understandable questions—and yet, more than 20,000 people across our state signed up to do this work with Powered by People, helping to register more than 260,000 new Texas voters and bringing hundreds of thousands more into the conversation around voting rights. Some even joined us and the Poor People's Campaign on a thirty-mile march from Georgetown, Texas, to Austin in 2021 to call for full voting rights for every eligible Texan. And we were far from the only group. Luci Baines Johnson, President Johnson's daughter, helped organize the Texas Right to Vote network, continuing her family's legacy of protecting the right to vote by bringing together faith leaders, civic organizations, and concerned Texans to the work of saving our democracy.

The volunteers who have signed up with Powered by People are doing tough work. It entails knocking on the doors of complete strangers and engaging in the kind of conversations that we aren't used to having—about voting and elections and our ability to be part of our government. That's no easy feat these days, when we are constantly distracted by the sensational and superficial; entranced by our personal digital devices; consumed by our own feed of like-minded social media connections; and disconnected from those who don't readily agree with us or share our immediate perspective.

But talking to people face-to-face is still the most powerful way to connect.

WE'VE GOT TO TRY

When I was running for Congress in 2012 against the incumbent, outspent and against the odds, I made it my mission to talk to as many voters directly, at their doors, as I could. Over the course of that campaign, I had countless conversations with those who had the power to decide the outcome. I didn't need a pollster to tell me what mattered most to El Paso voters when I could talk to those voters themselves.

I knew we might win that election when a guy approached me in a restaurant in Northeast El Paso. It was close to Election Day, and at this point, I had knocked on more than sixteen thousand doors.

"Are you Beto O'Rourke?" he asked me. "Because last week you knocked on my grandmother's door. She invited you in and told you about her great-grandson who is in the marines and her daughter who is a schoolteacher, and you all must have had a great conversation, because when I, and my thirty or so cousins, came to her house for menudo on Sunday, she made each of us promise to vote for you.

"You're going to win this thing," he told me.

Not every conversation at every door goes so well. I've also been yelled at, had doors slammed in my face, encountered dogs who were intent on taking a bite out of me before I could meet their owners. I've had long stretches, street after street, where it seems that no one is interested. It can make you feel like you don't have a chance.

But if you keep pushing, you'll find that person who's been waiting for you to come, waiting to tell you their story, waiting to hear yours.

That persistence won the day in 2012. Despite polls suggesting we'd lose that race, we won without a runoff in a five-person field that included the incumbent congressman.

I've applied that lesson to everything I've done since then, from getting legislation passed in Congress by trying to work with nearly

45

every member of the Republican majorities on my committees to going to each of the 254 counties of Texas when I ran for Senate in 2018.

Sometimes, the only way to avoid succumbing to the odds is to keep moving right through them. That's what these volunteers all over Texas understand. They've given us cause for hope in an otherwise hopeless situation.

Action, it turns out, is the antidote to despair.

We are fighting the biggest clampdown on democracy since 1965. And there is no guarantee that we will be able to overcome it. But for those of good conscience, who understand that this moment will determine whether we have a democracy at all going forward, there is no other choice. We've got to try.

We also take encouragement from remembering that Lawrence Nixon faced much longer odds and was up against not just the machinery of state government but the machinations of the Klan and other violent extremists who had proven that they would exact revenge by murdering and maiming those who would stand up for their rights and their humanity.

If Nixon and others like him could persist despite those threats, we can certainly do our part now that we have the chance. His example proves that not only is it necessary but that ultimately it pays off.

I've traveled Texas as a member of Congress, as a candidate, as an organizer, and as a voter registrar, and I have found Nixon's spirit alive and well. Whether it's fighting for the right to vote, or everything that the right to vote makes possible—like being able to see a doctor, or sending your kid to a good school, or having a reasonable expectation that you'll be treated equally under the law, or just getting something closer to a full understanding of our history—people across this state are doing the work. From Cotulla and South Texas to Fort Stockton and the Trans-Pecos; from Fort Bend in the southeast to Cooke County in the north; people are setting the example in their communities for what it will take for us as a state and as a country to come through.

On July 22, 1944, twenty years almost to the day from when he first stood up against the white primary in Texas, Lawrence Nixon and his wife, Drusilla, walked the three blocks from his office on Myrtle to Fire Station No. 5 and showed their poll tax receipts.

This time, they voted.

PART II

3

Cooke County

I first visited Cooke County as a Senate candidate in June 2018. It's rural and small, population 41,257. And it was the last of the 254 counties of Texas that I visited.

We held a big event to commemorate the occasion at another historic train depot, the Santa Fe station in Gainesville, the county seat. By this point, our campaign was really picking up steam, and if people knew one thing about how we were running our campaign it was that I was going to visit every county in Texas. So with Cooke being the 254th, there was a lot of buildup, a lot of media attention, and the turnout was beyond anything we could have hoped for. Hundreds packed the depot, and many more stood outside to listen to the speeches and music through the open windows.

Patriotic bunting adorned the windowsills. A band kept everyone loose and happy. A giant cake was brought out, with "Happy 254th!" written in bright red icing. The crowd of people, full of dogs and kids, was buzzing, almost bursting, with enthusiasm.

In a good mood, our campaign team had lunch at the fried pie restaurant before walking over to the depot. I grabbed a cherry pie to go and met up with Sherman Hartley Moore on the way over to the event.

I first met Sherman at a town hall meeting in a community theater in Graham, a small community two hours west of Dallas. A tall, thin guy with a bright, engaging face, he stood out right away. And when he got up from his seat to speak in that theater, his booming voice and forthright manner told me he wasn't just along for the ride. Sherman wasn't waiting for things to happen. It was clear from our first meeting that he was going to make them happen.

I felt like he could have been a kindred spirit to Woody Guthrie, who had worked, sung, and tramped through many of these same Texas towns in the 1920s and '30s and who had a fierce pride in the people who called them home. He stood up and sang for the marginalized and the downcast, the people out of power and far from the centers of it.

Sherman told me about all the towns we needed to visit, the places so often overlooked, taken for granted, and written off. He was ready to organize meetings, reach out to people, spread the word, and create opportunity where others saw none.

"If you'll make a stand out here in rural Texas," he said, "I'll be with you every step of the way." He was frustrated with Democrats looking past the small towns and out-of-the-way places. So was I. I told him I'd make the stand with him.

Sherman was true to his word, and from that point forward, he worked to connect me with rural communities throughout the state. In fact, it was Sherman who had put on the event in Gainesville.

As I ate my pie and walked toward the depot, he gave me a run-down of the dignitaries who would be there and the folks I should acknowledge in my speech, and provided me with a little bit of color on the history of Gainesville.

"Something you should know, Beto: Part of Truman's whistle-stop tour in 1948 came through Texas. In fact, he started the Texas trip in your hometown of El Paso and it ended right here in Gaines-ville at this depot we're walking up to." Sherman made the point that Truman was a fellow underdog. He wasn't expected to beat Dewey, but he met the odds with tenacity and a smiling confidence that ultimately carried the day.

A line of his came to mind. "America," Truman had said, "was not built on fear. America was built on courage, imagination, and an unbeatable determination to do the job at hand."

I always liked that one, a reminder that at our best, Americans are not afraid. We are not only doggedly optimistic but willing to do the work to realize that optimism.

Sherman continued, "The other thing you should know is that in 1944, an entire division of young army recruits trained in the fields just outside the city limits. After a few months, they boarded trains at this same Santa Fe train station and those trains took them to ships that would cross the Atlantic for England. And on D-Day, all of these boys who'd trained here in Cooke County boarded the troop transports that would ferry them across the Channel and land them on the beaches of Normandy. Every single one of them went over. But a lot of them never came home."

I let that sink in as I walked into the depot and joined the crowd to listen to the introductory speakers. This county that I hadn't known much about suddenly started to take on a significance for me that I hadn't expected.

I'd tell that story about the men who boarded those trains in Gainesville for the rest of the campaign. I'd tell folks that, regardless of whether those young men in 1944 were Republicans or Democrats, big-city kids or rural farmers, they stepped up to fight fascism and defend our democracy half a world away and they did it with the spirit of America Truman had described—unafraid and focused on the job at hand.

That was what defined Cooke County and Gainesville for me: fried pies, selfless service, and the most patriotic aspects of American character. But my next visit to Gainesville gave me a more complicated and honest understanding of the city and this country.

It was 2021, and I was traveling the state to help register voters and organize action across Texas to protect the right to vote, which was under attack in the aftermath of the *Shelby* decision.

The Voting Rights Act required jurisdictions that had historically suppressed the vote to submit any future changes to procedures or policies surrounding elections to the Justice Department before enactment. At the time of *Shelby*, seven of the Southern states, Alaska, and Arizona were covered in their entirety, with a number of counties in another five states (North Carolina, California, Florida, South Dakota, and New York) and two Michigan townships also subject to this oversight. In the decade before *Shelby*, the attorney general reviewed fourteen thousand to twenty thousand voting changes a year, rejecting any that ended up being discriminatory. Since the decision, the Justice Department has no longer had this authority, and what we've seen is devastating: hundreds of polling places have been closed in Texas; draconian ID laws have been implemented; and the art of gerrymandering has increasingly drawn minority voters into districts where the power and likelihood of their vote were significantly diminished.

But as bad as the past seven years had been, 2021 promised to be much worse. Donald Trump, trafficking in lies and conspiracy theories about the 2020 election, had induced a fixation on "voter fraud" among Republican legislators across the country, including in Texas. Despite the fact that Texans were statistically more likely to be struck by lightning than show up to a polling location and vote illegally, the state's GOP-controlled legislature was moving ahead with a bill that would further severely restrict voting access for low-income Texans, the disabled, and minority voters throughout the state. There was even a provision that would allow Texas to overturn the results of future elections simply based on the allegation of fraud.

I was intent on fighting this by helping to organize pro-democracy Texans wherever I could find them. I traveled to bright red towns like Midland and Abilene, Wichita Falls and Brenham (in Washington County), as well as reliably blue cities like Houston, Dallas, and Austin to enlist people to fight for the right to vote for everyone. And I also made it my mission to lead the way by trying to register as many people as I could, hoping to set an example that would be picked up by others.

I'd sometimes tell the story of Lawrence Nixon and his fight for voting rights at our events, making sure we all understood that this fight is not a new one, nor is it unwinnable. With the right combination of courage and "unbeatable determination," we could get it done.

Stopping the attempt at voter suppression in Texas was the most urgent priority. Registering more voters was the insurance policy in case we failed. I figured if we couldn't un-rig the system, we could at least add a lot more people to the rolls and see if hundreds of thousands of new voters could overcome the obstacles the legislature was placing in our way.

At the beginning of 2021, there were more than three million eligible Texans who were not registered to vote. That's not by accident, but by design. In Texas, there is no automatic voter registration, no same-day voter registration, and it's one of only ten states that do not allow you to register online. And to make it even more challenging, if you want to help someone get registered, you have to become a certified volunteer deputy registrar, which, in most counties, requires you to make a trip to the courthouse to be trained and tested by the county's elections department.

So that's exactly what I was doing in Cooke County, organizing folks around voting rights and getting myself certified as a volunteer deputy registrar so I could legally go out and register more people to vote.

It was a rainy June morning and I pulled up in front of the courthouse annex to get sworn in, three years to the day from my last visit. But before I walked into the county registrar's office, I stopped to admire the main county courthouse across the street.

Built in 1911, right around the time the beaux arts craze in American public architecture was coming to an end, the squat limestone and brick courthouse sits on California Street, a marker commemorating its importance as a stop on the California trail, "blazed by the pioneers of '49."

But as I continued to walk around the grounds, shrugging off the rain and the looks I got from folks who were scurrying inside to escape the weather, I was struck by another monument, this one far more prominent and imposing.

The Confederate Soldiers and Sailors statue defines the northeast corner of the courthouse grounds. Facing north and standing two stories tall, the monument was erected the same year that the courthouse was built and is emblazoned with encomiums to the Lost Cause:

"God holds the scales of justice; he will measure praise and blame; and the South will stand the verdict; and will stand it without shame." (Source unknown.)

And,

"Oh home of tears, but let her bear this blazoned to the end of time; no nation rose so white and fair, none fell so pure of crime." (From a dedication inscribed by English poet Philip Stanhope Worsley to Robert E. Lee in Worsley's translation of Homer's *Iliad*.)

And, lest Confederate women be forgotten,

"To the women of the Confederacy, whose pious ministrations to our wounded soldiers and sailors soothed the last hours of those who died far from the objects of their tenderest love; and whose patriotism will teach their children to emulate the deeds of their revolutionary sires."

Their revolutionary sires!

As I would later learn, part of what makes this imposing monument to the Confederate States of America so interesting is that in 1861, when Texas held a referendum on secession, Cooke County actually voted *against* joining the Confederacy. Slaveholders were a powerful but small minority in the North Texas community, and most residents wanted to focus on their farms and families, not on protecting the interests of plantation owners or defending the institution of slavery.

Even more unpopular was a conscription mandate the following year. The idea that most of the county's men would be sent to fight distant battles for a cause they didn't believe in, leaving their land untended and their families undefended from Indian raids, was inconceivable to these folks. Adding insult to injury, the slaveholders in Cooke County were largely exempted from the draft. Discontent spread, and thirty of Cooke's citizens sent a petition of protest to the Confederate government in Richmond.

This growing unrest, and an unconfirmed plot to raid the arsenal in Cooke County, caused the Confederate provost marshal for northern Texas, Colonel James Bourland, to order the arrest of more than 150 county residents, all of them white men, who had failed to report for military duty.

A "citizens court" with a slaveholder-majority jury was quickly stood up, convicting seven of the defendants of treason. They were hanged within a week of judgment. But the pro-Confederate mob, paranoid about the alleged threat posed by Unionist sympathizers and immigrants from neighboring pro-Union states, demanded more. Soon, fourteen additional men were selected and hanged, one or two at a time, from the same old tree as the first seven. And after unknown assassins killed two of the local Confederate leaders, another nineteen men were selected from the original 150 and hanged. Two others were shot trying to escape.

All told, forty-two men were killed by their neighbors and fellow citizens, making Gainesville the site of the largest mass hanging in U.S. history. (It is worth noting that two months after the "Great Hanging at Gainesville," President Abraham Lincoln ordered the executions of thirty-eight Dakota men following a similar sham trial at the conclusion of the 1862 Dakota War. Brutality and inhumanity were not the exclusive purview of Confederates or Texans. All thirty-eight Native American men were hanged from a giant scaffold built for the occasion.)

For 152 years after the hanging at Gainesville, there was no plaque or marker in the community explaining what had happened, the story of this atrocity and the names of the victims unknown to the people of Cooke County, the history missing from classrooms and textbooks—until members of the community finally convinced Gainesville to put up a memorial in 2014, with the names of the forty-two men who had been murdered.

For more than a century, it was instead a Confederate monument that had pride of place at the courthouse, even though Cooke's citizens had voted against joining the Confederacy, disregarding the inconvenient truth that one of the greatest atrocities committed by the Confederacy in Texas was against the very people of this county.

And it wasn't the only Confederate statue in town.

As if the people of Gainesville in the early twentieth century were desperate to rebrand themselves as loyal Confederate partisans, or perhaps to remind everyone about who belonged in power and who did not, there was another imposing monument to the Lost Cause, at the main city park, the same one where we'd scheduled our town hall meeting on democracy and voting rights.

Donated to the city by the local chapter of the Daughters of the Confederacy in 1908, this other Confederate statue dominated the entrance to Leonard Park.

But unlike the courthouse monument, this one was coming down.

There was no hoopla, no bands or bunting, no cheering crowd on this cold rainy day as we gathered under the park's portico. But I did have Sherman Moore. He took the mic and introduced me to the seventy people who showed up to talk about voting rights and the state of our democracy. True to his word, he had my back there in rural Texas, despite the fact that I wasn't running for anything this time. I was there to organize, to register voters, to engage with Texans who often get overlooked.

As the town hall came to a close, I reminded the folks that I was a newly minted volunteer deputy registrar, street legal in Cooke County, and could help anyone interested to get on the rolls. A young woman named Jenika Ragsdale introduced herself and took me up on the offer. As I was helping her with the registration form, I mentioned the Confederate monuments at the courthouse and the park.

"Well, we're working on it," she told me.

She shared that there was a group she's part of called PRO Gainesville and that they'd made it their mission to bring these Confederate statues down. They had recently marched to protest the one at the courthouse and three of her colleagues were arrested.

I asked her why.

"They got them for not staying on the sidewalk and walking in the parallel parking lane."

They weren't issued tickets, they weren't given a warning; instead, they were arrested and briefly jailed. But the arrests didn't deter them. They tried again, this time making their case in front of the city council. And it worked: the town agreed to remove the statue at Leonard Park.

It's a testament not just to these young organizers but to the council members who heard them and acted courageously. The protesters were the catalyst, but those in positions of public trust took that spark and converted it into lasting change for their community. It renewed my faith in our democracy, and my pride in the people of Gainesville and Cooke County. When called to serve the highest ideals of our country, they came through.

It's a story as old as our democracy: civil rights leaders pushing those in high office to listen to the uncomfortable truth, to care about those so often overlooked or written off.

That's what the marchers in Selma did: they gave President Johnson "the power" to pass a voting rights bill.

That's what Jenika and her colleagues were doing in Gainesville. That's what I've found people all over Texas doing, people like Courtney Ratliff in Midland.

———

Later that summer, our voting rights campaign brought us to the Permian Basin. Founded and named as the halfway between Fort Worth and El Paso, Midland and its sister city Odessa are best known as the hub for the Permian Basin oil and gas industry.

We had gathered in Booker T. Washington Park one evening in early June. I remember a beautiful sky and a few hundred people who'd come out to talk about how we were going to protect our democracy. As I got out of my truck, I saw a woman who had just gotten home from her shift as a nurse at a local hospital. I could tell she was tired, but I took a chance and introduced myself. She told me her name was Dee.

"What are you-all doing in the park?" she asked, pointing to the gathering across the street.

"We're working to make sure everyone can vote!" I answered. "You should come join us."

I walked into the gathering of people from Midland and Odessa, as well as those who came from Big Spring, Monahans, Andrews, and Rankin. We talked about what had brought us out, thanked one another for committing ourselves to the fight, and got ready to hear from the speakers.

But before that happened, someone introduced me to Courtney Ratliff, a Midland schoolteacher. "You've gotta meet this guy. If you're interested in democracy, he's figured out how to make it work!"

"All right," I said, turning to Courtney, "you've gotta tell me your story."

Courtney shared with me that in the wake of George Floyd's murder, he decided to help lead his community to rename one of the last Robert E. Lee High Schools in Texas, which happened to be in Midland.

The city fathers of Midland only named the school in 1961—a hundred years after the start of the Civil War, forty years after the heyday of the Klan in Texas, and just as African Americans in Texas began to make gains in civil rights. *Brown v. Board of Education* had been decided just seven years earlier. The year before, four students from North Carolina A&T College had sat in at the Woolworth's in Greensboro. And in 1961, Freedom Riders were testing the limits of the Constitution for integrated interstate travel.

There had been no Midland, Texas, when Robert E. Lee was alive, no deep connection to the Confederacy in the Permian Basin.

The impetus for the name might have had more to do with the fact that Midland was one of the last school districts in the state of Texas to comply with *Brown v. Board of Education* and integrate public education, forced to do so by court order.

The school board at the time, forced to desegregate against their will, decided they'd enact a price, Courtney explained: "Okay, we're going to name the school that these young Black kids are going to go to after Robert E. Lee. Your mascot is going to be the Rebels. Your school flag is going to be the Confederate battle flag. And your school band is going to play 'Dixie' after every touchdown."

Courtney had taught at Robert E. Lee as an assistant band director. I asked him what that meant to him, as a Black man, to be teaching students who might not appreciate the full history contained in the name of their school.

"I taught in that school for a year; it was my first experience right out of college. We were playing a football game against the Dallas Kimball Knights—a predominantly African American school. When the Kimball band officers came over to greet our band, my director decided to dedicate a song to them and chose 'Cotton Fields.' I saw the faces of my students all looking at me at once, with some of them mouthing, 'Mr. Ratliff, we cannot play this song for them.' The kids realized what we were doing. Later, I asked my director why we had done that. He said it was spur of the moment—that Kimball had the championship football team, but he wanted to show off our award-winning band and this was one song he knew they could play without advance notice."

In 1989, the school stopped flying the Confederate flag. In 2017, they stopped playing "Dixie." But changing the name was the last important step to take.

They had put their all into two previous attempts, but were unable to rally enough support to convince the school board. It was tough, it might have even seemed hopeless, but they had to keep trying.

The third attempt turned out to be the charm—led by those who wrote hundreds of letters and emails to the school board on a daily basis, who reached out to family and friends to engage them in the campaign, who, just like Lawrence Nixon, had the courage to keep the faith. Together, they convinced the board that it was time.

And like the Gainesville City Council, those board members did the courageous thing and changed the name, in a 6–1 vote, to Legacy High School. The people gave those trustees the power, and they used it.

"People finally decided that Midland can do better," Ratliff told me.

He also told me he'd received some threats and been harassed along the way. But he felt that the effort and the outcome were worth the hardship and the sacrifice.

"I'm so glad those kids don't have to go through this anymore," he told me.

I thanked Courtney and turned my attention to those leading the meeting at the park. Soon, the speeches began and we each took turns talking about why democracy was worth fighting for and worth saving. We committed ourselves to the work ahead, no matter how hard it would be.

As I gave my remarks to the people who'd come out under that beautiful West Texas sky, I saw Dee, the nurse from across the street.

She gave me a thumbs-up, ready to do her part.

———

Back in Gainesville, Jenika told me that while the Confederate monument in front of us was about to come down, it hadn't been easy. But she knew why she had to keep trying. "I grew up a mixed girl in Texas. My dad was a second-generation Mexican American. Once I had children of my own, I knew I had to try to change at least our part of the world to make life better for them than it was for me." At several key moments, she and her colleagues had to look up from defeat and find a way to keep moving forward.

"We pushed the county commissioners court to pull down the

statue in front of the courthouse, but we couldn't get them to change their minds. So we turned our attention to the city council because they have say over the parks. And after protesting and showing up to council meetings and organizing our fellow citizens, this Confederate statue will finally be coming down this summer."

The citizens of Gainesville had been able to pull off a victory denied to every person who'd tried before them for the last 110 years. It was a feat of civic leadership, a resounding confirmation of the power of our democracy. People peacefully, nonviolently organized to put an end to the public praise of those who'd violently attacked our democracy in the past. They help us to understand that we can never condone, encourage, or celebrate sedition, whether it occurred in 1861 or 2021.

And yet—the reason we were talking in the first place is that she wasn't even registered to vote.

Jenika apparently saw more promise and power in direct organizing than she did at the ballot box. Or maybe it's the fact that it's harder than it needs to be to register to vote in Texas. At any rate, I helped her get registered and suggested that in addition to voting in future elections, there was even more she could do.

"What about running to serve as a county commissioner, so that you're the one making the decisions for this community?"

She told me she'd think about it.

4

Pecos County

It was early August 2017 and I was on the trail with my family in West Texas. We'd just picked the kids up from camp in Jeff Davis County a few days before, and they were joining Amy and me on a few campaign stops in Fort Davis, Alpine, and Marfa.

Soon afterward, we pulled into the city of Fort Stockton, in Pecos County, without a planned event on the schedule, since it was supposed to be a rest day. But while the kids jumped in the hotel pool, I told the campaign team I thought we should organize an impromptu town hall meeting at the local Dickey's barbecue restaurant. I recorded a quick video on Twitter and Facebook urging people in the area to come out. Around dinnertime, Amy and I gathered the kids, piled them back into the truck, and showed up to greet all the people who'd come to meet us.

But when we got to the Dickey's, no supporters were waiting. No voters were wanting to ask me questions. No one. In fact, the only person in the restaurant was the manager—an immigrant from India, who was grateful we'd chosen his restaurant to hold our (so far) sparsely attended town hall meeting. I told him not to worry, folks would be here soon. In the meantime, I asked him for a recommendation about what to order.

"I'm a vegetarian," he said. "But everyone seems to like the brisket."

We took his advice, ate, and waited for people to show up. Eventually, we got a robust crowd of ten or twelve—essentially three families, one of which was just passing through Pecos County when they saw my video and decided to pull in off the main road. The county judge, Joe Shuster, also came out.

Now, finally, we had a real meeting on our hands.

I was no stranger to town hall meetings. When I served on the El Paso City Council, I held one every Monday morning for six years. I'd lay out what would be on Tuesday's council agenda, answer questions, hear what people had to say about changes they wanted to see in their neighborhoods, or listen to their ideas about issues—like how we were going to create more jobs or preserve more acres of public land.

Sometimes I'd have a guest speaker, like the director of the streets department or the city manager. These weekly meetings made me a lot better at my job than I would have been otherwise. I knew I'd have to study that agenda carefully to make sure I could answer any question that came my way. I also knew I'd have to explain every one of my votes to my constituents the following Monday. It introduced a level of accountability that kept me focused on those I was elected to serve.

I did the same thing as a member of Congress, holding a monthly town hall meeting for the general public and a quarterly town hall meeting for veterans. It was all comers welcomed, no holds barred. Anyone could ask any question, level any criticism, offer any idea. I'd stay until the last person had their say. One time we kept the meeting going in the parking lot after getting kicked out of the high school auditorium because we'd been there for more than three hours and the custodian wanted to lock up and go home.

Just like the town hall meetings I held when I was on the city council, these congressional town halls made me a better representative. I had to justify my votes and what I was doing with this position of public trust. I couldn't come back with excuses. I might have been a Democrat in a Republican-majority chamber, but that could never justify a lack of progress.

These meetings kept me laser-focused on my community and the people I served. They also produced a lot of helpful conversations. When veterans shared with me the challenges of trying to get an appointment at the local VA, I could use these details to help make significant changes that improved wait times and outcomes for them. I proposed legislation in Congress that was literally written in dialogue with community members on issues ranging from benefits for returning service members, to preservation of public lands, to improving immigration laws for the family members of U.S. citizens.

Some of these bills passed and some didn't—but they all came from the community I represented and were all made possible by the open, honest conversations in these town hall meetings.

So I was looking forward to this impromptu town hall in Fort Stockton. I knew I'd learn something and come away a better candidate and a better person for it.

I shook everyone's hand, told them how glad I was they came out, and expressed my gratitude to Dickey's for hosting us and for their brisket, which turned out to be excellent. But before I could get much further, one of the attendees, a woman from Fort Stockton, stood up and asked:

"What are you going to do about Obamacare?"

She told me that she made too much to qualify for Medicaid but not enough to afford any of the plans on the Affordable Care Act exchange.

"Me and my spouse are lower middle class. We're not able to afford health care. So we bypass that. We have to make the decision: Do we put food on the table or do we buy insurance that we probably won't be able to use because, what doctor are you going to see here? Sometimes you have to travel hundreds of miles to see a doctor."

I began to explain that because Texas had refused Medicaid expansion, even though the federal government would initially cover 100 percent of the cost, she was one of the millions of Texans left in the lurch. In fact, we were the least-insured state in the country, one where people died of diabetes, the flu, and curable cancers, all because our elected leaders wanted to make a symbolic stand against President Obama more than they wanted to save the lives of the people they represented.

"It doesn't matter if they expand Medicaid," she countered. "In a place like Fort Stockton, no doctor takes Medicare or Medicaid. I'll never get the help I need. I'll just keep working hard while the people who don't take the benefits."

We continued the conversation and I told her that even if we didn't agree on every issue, including health care, it was important that we kept listening to each other. I told her that I appreciated her joining us and challenging me in a forum like this.

"This may not be easy or comfortable," I told her, "but listening to each other is what we need to be doing."

She agreed. "A lot of people, they just agree and shake their head and say 'yes' and just go with the flow. We have to have somebody that's going to stand up and ruffle things up and move things in the right direction for everybody, not just certain people."

And then, something pretty amazing happened. A young man, one of the few other people in the room, stood up and introduced himself. "I'm a doctor practicing here in Fort Stockton," he said. "I accept Medicaid and Medicare. In fact, I'd be happy to see you, even if you don't have insurance."

If I'd had any doubts about the wisdom of holding a town hall meeting in Fort Stockton that day, or holding campaign events that were so open and unstructured, where really anything could happen, that moment answered my concerns. What was taking place before us was really special. We were bringing people together, folks whose paths might not otherwise cross, to have some tough but productive conversations. And we were also connecting people who could actually help each other, like this doctor who was going to be able to take care of this woman—a neighbor of his he'd never met and probably never would have met—who'd been forced to choose between putting food on the table and buying health insurance.

After the town hall was over, I introduced myself to the doctor and asked him to tell me his story. "I grew up here, graduated from high school here," Auden Velasquez told me. "And I wanted to go to medical school, but there was no way I could afford it." He motioned to Judge Shuster to come over. "But the judge found a way to help me out."

Shuster shared with me how he and the commissioners court decided to pay for half of Velasquez's medical school education and, thanks to the Outstanding Rural Scholar Recognition Program, the state of Texas would pick up the other half. They did this on the condition that after becoming a doctor, Velasquez would return to Fort Stockton and practice medicine for a minimum of six years.

In other words, the community would invest in his success if he'd commit to serving the town that made his success possible. The kicker: by the time I'd met him, he had already satisfied his six-year requirement and was in his eighth year in Fort Stockton, with no plans to leave. He'd married a hometown girl and they were raising their family together there.

He was focusing on the people he'd grown up with, the people who'd nurtured him and literally guaranteed his success by underwriting his education. For the bargain price of just medical school tuition, Pecos County got a homegrown doctor to take care of the people of the community.

What Joe Shuster did to address the needs of his community really made an impression on me. The creativity, the dedication, the fact that he was so personally invested in Velasquez's success—that's a real public servant in my book.

Unfortunately, the state program that Shuster used to grow more hometown doctors no longer exists. That's too bad, because if ever there was a time to invest in more health care workers, it's now. And if ever there was a place that needed them, it's rural Texas.

I came back to Fort Stockton in 2021 and had the chance to meet with Judge Shuster and Dr. Velasquez again, along with some other local health care leaders, to see how they were doing. These were tough times. Covid, and the resulting strain of delivering care without enough doctors or hospital beds, had proved too much for some.

Fort Stockton, like much of the country, had been hit hard by the pandemic. The county hospital quickly filled up and because other parts of Texas were struggling as well, they were forced to transfer patients to Arkansas and New Mexico. They were short on supplies, ventilators, and providers. Nurses were forced to work outside of their scope of practice.

Dr. Velasquez told me that, for the first time in his career, he felt like quitting.

"I had patients die. I had to tell an eighteen-year-old kid that his fifty-two-year-old father had died. And I just felt like I couldn't do anything."

Compounding these challenges is the fact that Texas is also experiencing a staffing shortage in the health care industry. Big Bend Regional Health Center, for instance, covers a twelve-thousand-square-mile area that serves twenty-five thousand people, but since February 2021, more than half of their physician workforce had left the area.

Why?

According to Dr. Adrian Billings, one of the center's family physicians, the answer is Covid. And stress. And not having enough other providers to help.

"It's like running a marathon at a sprint," he told me.

The half of workers who left still haven't been replaced—leaving not just Fort Stockton and Pecos County, but also smaller surrounding communities like Presidio, which is on the border with Mexico in Brewster County, underserved. Dr. Linda Molinar told me that health care access was already so bad in Presidio that, because there was no doctor in town, her brother had been delivered by the town's veterinarian. Like the folks in Pecos County, she is trying to solve the problem by encouraging local students—including her son—to pursue medical education.

But no longer able to depend on the canceled Rural Scholar program, her family has had to work hard to find the resources to get her son the education he and his community will need for their mutual success. He's the exception, she said. Because rural communities are so medically underserved, it's rare for kids in these communities to ever *see* a doctor. And therefore, they just don't realize that it's possible for them to someday *be* a doctor.

"The vast majority of the kids you see in medical school these days are from the big cities and suburbs," she told me.

She suggested the state start a program that would target rural students for recruitment to medical school. I said I thought that was a great idea.

Dr. Billings told me that in the short term the solution is "expanding Medicaid, bringing in these federal funds so that local money can be used for . . ."

"For survival," Judge Shuster said, finishing his sentence.

In fact, as of 2019, more than 30 of Texas's 254, predominantly rural counties do not have even a single doctor. More than twenty other counties have only one. Seventy-one counties do not have a hospital. And many, like Pecos, are having to cut services like obstetrics to be able to stretch limited resources further and deliver basic services to more people.

And of course, this doesn't affect only rural communities.

As residents of the least-insured state in the country, Texans across the state struggle to see a doctor or a mental-health-care provider. They can't fill their prescriptions or go to therapy.

In Laredo back in 2017, I met a young man named Joey. Twenty-nine years old at the time, he told me he had diabetes and glaucoma. Because he was uninsured, he hadn't been treated for thirteen years, because he couldn't afford the medication. The one time he'd seen a doctor, at a federally qualified health center that provides care on a sliding scale for those without insurance, Joey was told that he'd be dead before he turned forty if he didn't start taking the medicine he needed.

There is a perverse irony in the fact that the expansion of this lifesaving program is being denied in the state that produced the man who signed Medicaid into law in the first place. Lyndon Johnson did this on July 30, 1965, eight days before signing the Voting Rights Act, which underscores how central Texas has been in the critical fights for basic rights, like the right to have medical care and the right to vote.

Growing up in precarious financial circumstances himself, and working for people who came from even humbler origins, Johnson understood from his own life experiences just how important health care was to any prospect of success in life. No one should be too poor, too old, too politically unconnected to see a doctor. And fortunately, he felt the same way about voting.

Edna McIver, Dr. Lawrence Nixon's youngest daughter, grew up in the house on Myrtle Avenue in El Paso, the same one from which Nixon would walk the three blocks to the polling station each election. She remembers the good old days, when the cattle drives still came down their street, shaking the homes, tearing down her neighbors' fences. A time when her father and other doctors still made house calls, taking care of everyone in the neighborhood, including Black, Latino, and white patients.

"Daddy never charged anyone more than two dollars for an office visit and never more than four dollars to visit them at home."

Edna said that when colleagues encouraged him to charge more, Nixon would push back with "How are these folks going to survive if everyone charges them as much as they can?"

He wasn't the only Texan who thought like this. More than a decade before Medicaid became law, Oveta Culp Hobby was named the first secretary of Health, Education, and Welfare by President Dwight Eisenhower. From Killeen, Texas, and married to former Texas governor William Hobby, Culp Hobby initially worried that social welfare programs had become too generous following the Roosevelt and Truman administrations.

But ultimately, she saw the benefit of expanding social insurance programs as a means of helping people to become more self-reliant. It's hard to pull yourself up by your bootstraps if you're too sick or in too much pain to do so. In fact, it was a man on Culp Hobby's team, Wilbur Cohen, who would ultimately pilot the successful effort to get Medicare and Medicaid passed into law under President Johnson.

And yet, despite Medicaid's Texas roots, we are one of the few states to reject Medicaid expansion. That leaves an estimated 766,000 people in the Medicaid "coverage gap," meaning that they earn too little to qualify for an Affordable Care Act subsidy but too much to meet the stringent requirements for Medicaid enrollment in Texas. Just like the woman I met in the Dickey's restaurant in Fort Stockton.

The gap is larger than you might think. If you are disabled or have children and earn $150 a month or less ($300 per month for a family), you qualify for Medicaid in Texas. If you make more than that, you are out of luck. Roughly 20 percent of the state's thirty million people don't have health insurance.

Those in the coverage gap don't regularly see a doctor, don't get medication, and don't receive any kind of preventative health care. When they do see a provider, it's often in the emergency room, where outcomes are going to be worse and much more expensive than they would have been with care delivered preventatively. And because these patients are uninsured, it is society as a whole that will end up footing the bill—premiums go up, hospital costs go up, local hospital district tax rates go up. Whatever additional expense is involved in increasing coverage, it pales in comparison to the costs of treating the uninsured.

And it turns out the cost to expand coverage in Texas is close to nothing. After the Affordable Care Act was passed in 2010, the federal government offered Texas the opportunity to expand Medicaid for an initial cost of zero dollars. Literally, the feds would pick up 100 percent of the bill, moving down to 90 percent over time. Texas rejected the deal.

In the more than ten years since, Texas has left more than one hundred billion dollars on the table. That's money that would have kept people from dying premature deaths. One hundred billion dollars that could have kept more rural hospitals open, attracted more providers to underserved communities, and reduced the property tax bills that underwrite uncompensated care in Texas. That's a lot of good that we've forgone.

But that doesn't have to be our future or our fate.

In 2021, Julie Johnson in the Texas House and Nathan Johnson in the Texas Senate introduced a Medicaid expansion bill on Texas terms. More conservative than the kinds of expansion seen in other

states, their bill contained strong incentives for work and other qualifications that answered concerns raised by their Republican colleagues, including the fear that the federal government might one
day pull back its share of funding. The legislation included an "opt-
out" for Texas if that were ever to happen.

They were able to secure support from many House Republicans,
business groups, and local governments across Texas. Even more important, polls conducted during that legislative session showed that
the vast majority of Texans—a full 70 percent—wanted it.

All of this produced the broad political will necessary to pass the
bill in the House, where there were commitments from a majority
of legislators to vote in favor. But the chairs of committees in both
chambers blocked the bills from even getting a hearing. In other
words, a small number of Republican leaders blocked a bill popular
with Republicans and Democrats alike in the legislature and across
the state.

Though these party leaders might have won in the short term,
it's clear that there is broad bipartisan support to get this done—
eventually.

How long it takes is up to us. As soon as enough voters feel that
they can no longer sit by while people die unnecessary deaths or have
to choose between feeding themselves and filling their prescriptions,
we will elect leaders whose political will matches that of the people
they represent. It's also up to us to make sure that our democracy is
what it claims to be: government of, by, and for the people. *All* of the
people. There are a lot of potential voters out there, millions of them
in Texas, who have a hard time registering to vote or getting out to
the polls on election day and don't vote. Very often they are the ones
without insurance, struggling to make ends meet, for whom politics

might seem like a luxury that they can't afford. If you're making less than a living wage (in a state where the minimum is still $7.25 an hour!), you might be working two or even three jobs to make ends meet. If, on top of that, you're taking care of a sick kid or parent who doesn't have health care, when are you going to find time to go down to the courthouse to register to vote? And if you look up to see how badly gerrymandered your district is—meaning your chance of affecting the outcome of a state legislative race in November is truly marginal—you might just say to hell with it anyway. It's these potential voters who bear the brunt of the most stringent registration and voting laws in America (where you can't register online and where wait times to vote sometimes stretch for hours) and some of the most cynically drawn districts in the country. Their absence from the electorate has a lot to do with how we end up with these kinds of policy outcomes.

But democracy encompasses more than just the legislative choices made at one level of government. Judge Shuster and the commissioners court in Pecos responded to local pressures, opportunities, and accountability when they invested in Auden Velasquez's medical education.

It's so often the most local level of government that most accurately reflects Lincoln's idea of a republic that is "of the people, by the people, for the people." These are the folks—commissioners, school board trustees, city council members—who are likely to see their constituents on a daily basis, filling up at the gas station, buying groceries, dropping their kids off at school. They are the ones without intervening staff members who would otherwise insulate them from the demands of their fellow citizens. These are the local representatives who will be called by their constituents when their garbage doesn't get picked up, or when they have a sick family member who has to drive two hours to see a doctor, or when their son wants to go to medical school but can't pay for it.

I ran for the El Paso City Council in 2005. Though I had never run for office before, I had been involved in the business community and civic life of El Paso. I ran a small technology firm downtown, helping to create the kind of higher-wage technology jobs that our community needed if we were going to make El Paso a place where young people wanted to stay or move back to. I'd also started an on-line newspaper that covered city politics, the arts, and the binational relationship between El Paso and Ciudad Juárez.

This gave me a chance to serve on a number of local commissions and boards. As I became more engaged in the community, I started helping out on political campaigns, including for our state senator, Eliot Shapleigh, one of the first people I'd heard speak about El Paso in ambitious, aspirational terms. He was absolutely not interested in "good enough" for El Paso. He wanted us to be the best. Through Shapleigh, I met other aspiring leaders, like Veronica Escobar, who now represents our community in Congress, and Steve Ortega and Susie Byrd, who were also running for city council in 2005.

I knocked on doors all day, every day leading up to the election in 2005. I was running against the incumbent, who also happened to be mayor pro tem. Because I couldn't match him in spending or name recognition, I had to meet as many of the voters who would decide the outcome of that election as I could. I ended up winning that race, and Steve and Susie won theirs as well.

After that, we all became good friends and partners who worked on the issues that we'd heard about knocking on doors during the campaign. For example, people complained about the transit system—how old the buses were, how often they'd break down, how unreliable it was to depend on public transportation to get you to work or school or to see your family. In a town where a significant number of people didn't own a car, it became clear that fixing transit was key to our community's success.

We made significant investments in new buses, a new rapid transit system with dedicated lanes, and most important, a level of accountability that had not existed before. Within five years, El Paso's was named the best midsized transit system in the country.

In the midst of our work on the transit system and the subdivision code and other fundamental aspects of city life, our friend Carlos Gallinar invited us to meet some young men and women who were working in an alternative education and work program that he ran from a nonprofit in Segundo Barrio, the same neighborhood in which Nixon had first lived when he moved to El Paso a hundred years earlier. It turned into an impromptu town hall meeting, where the three of us answered questions from people we would otherwise probably never get a chance to hear from.

A young man named Sal asked me why, as a gay man, he was treated differently than other people he knew. Why, for example, could he not marry his boyfriend?

We talked about the fact that same-sex marriage had been prohibited in the state of Texas by statute and by constitutional amendment. That prohibition barred any political subdivision, including the city of El Paso, from doing the right thing and treating everyone equally.

Sal asked us to think about what else we might be able to do. As a young man who could live anywhere, he needed to know that the city of El Paso valued him or else he—and many others like him—would find opportunity elsewhere.

Steve, Susie, and I went back to city hall. We talked with city employees, learning about some of the challenges they faced. We heard a lot about how hard it was for gay employees to get health insurance for their partners if they weren't legally married.

Those conversations inspired an ordinance to offer health care benefits to the same-sex partners of city employees, just like married spouses received. We might not be able to change state law on marriage equality, but we could at least treat all city employees equally.

We presented it to our colleagues and made the case to the public. El Paso had always been a city that led on civil rights and human rights. We argued that we could not break with that proud tradition, nor could we afford to lose those who might leave El Paso because they weren't being treated equally.

The ordinance passed, but it provoked some intense opposition, especially from those who felt that the city council was condoning or promoting "immoral" behavior. The controversy over the health care benefits was still going after my second term ended in 2011 and I was no longer on the council. Groups attempted to recall Steve, Susie, and Mayor John Cook, and the issue became a lightning rod for Steve when he ran and lost a race for mayor in 2013.

There were also lawsuits, injunctions, and court settlements around the issue, with Cook racking up more than seven hundred thousand dollars in personal legal fees. But he and a slim majority of the council had the courage of their convictions and continued to support those city employees and the principle of equal treatment. It was a long, costly fight, but their ultimate victory not only protected city employees, it also signaled to the world that El Paso would continue to be a community that valued equality and fairness.

And it was only possible because, at the local level, El Paso was a functioning democracy—one whose representatives felt an obligation to meet the needs of the people they served.

———

These are the two sides of democracy in America. When it's broken, as is the case at the state level right now, you can't even pass commonsense policies like Medicaid expansion. After all, if Texas were functioning like a real democracy, would we turn down billions of dollars in federal money (really, our federal tax dollars coming back to us) to help our fellow Texans get the health care they need?

Or would we have a law on the books banning abortion at conception with no exception for rape or incest in a state that has one of the highest rates of maternal mortality in the country? After all, Texas is the state that produced the *Roe v. Wade* decision. Not only was the plaintiff, Norma McCorvey (known by the pseudonym "Jane Roe") from Texas, but so were the two attorneys who successfully pled her case and won the landmark decision that made abortion legal in the United States, Linda Coffee and Sarah Weddington.

This status quo of deeply harmful and unpopular policies is only possible because our representatives in Austin do not feel accountable to the people of Texas—both because of the gerrymandering that has insulated them from legitimate challengers and the suppression that has kept so many citizens away from the polls.

El Paso, on the other hand, like so many other cities, is closer to a real democracy, because our representatives are forced to interact with the folks who elected them to office in the first place. Meetings

83

take place every week and are open to the public. Anyone can walk into city hall and walk up to talk to their council member.

I know from experience that this produces a positive motivation to deliver for your community because you are constantly confronted with opportunities to improve people's lives—literally, to fix a pothole, or a streetlight, or a drainage system—as well as opportunities to improve the life of the community, like rewriting the subdivision code to encourage more parks, affordable housing, and sustainable development in the neighborhoods that we're building.

There's also a profound respect that you have for the people you serve, heightened by the public accountability that takes place at city council meetings and town halls, as well as in coffee shops, bars, and grocery stores. This is the motivation to not let people down, to make sure you come through on your commitments, to be able to deliver on the promises you've made.

That's why we were able to actually improve public transit, preserve open space for public recreation, balance the budget every year, and do so much more beyond that—because we had an accountable government. It also doesn't hurt that the elections for city council and mayor in El Paso are nonpartisan. Without an "R" or a "D" next to your name, there's one less divide to bridge as you build coalitions to get things done. It's amazing what you can accomplish when you don't define yourself by your differences from others.

In order for this country's democracy to really start working for us, it needs to learn from local governments, where elected officials are far more closely connected and responsive to the people they purport to represent. And whether or not this happens—whether we let a broken system break our spirit or we find a way to rise above it—comes down to us.

That means getting involved—taking stands at the local level, yes, but also demanding better of our state and federal governments. It means an end to partisan gerrymandering and adopting independent citizen-led redistricting commissions so our federal and state representatives aren't choosing their own voters. It means removing the barriers to full democratic participation, like adopting comprehensive voting rights reforms.

And we can also learn from an important change that El Paso citizens made to our city charter the year before I was elected to the council: term limits. Knowing that I would have no more than eight years to serve my community before I termed out forced me to think through exactly what I hoped to accomplish and introduced a greater urgency to my work than if I'd had the prospect of unlimited terms in front of me. Term limits are also an acknowledgment that in this great country no single one of us is indispensable or irreplaceable. It's a pledge of faith in our fellow citizens and in the diversity of our communities to commit to serving for a set period of time and then getting out of the way so that someone else can bring their unique experience, expertise, and perspective to bear on the pressing issues before us. It also has the added benefit of producing a government that looks a lot more like the people it's supposed to represent. When you have the same guy serving the same community in the same office for twenty, thirty, or even forty years, you're losing out on so much of the change and opportunity that has taken place there in that time.

To do all of this we must channel the resilience of Lawrence Nixon, who paid his poll tax year after year, even when he wasn't welcomed in America's democracy, because he wanted the world to know he wouldn't stop fighting until he was. That's the approach we need to have—voting in every single election, volunteering to bring more voters onto the rolls and into our elections, even as we acknowledge all the ways the system is designed to prop up the status quo, because we recognize that only through our participation can we overcome that and elect the people who reflect our values, who are ready and willing to make the changes necessary to ensure that our democracy more closely resembles the ideal of full citizen participation.

5

La Salle County

The city of Cotulla is a little more than an hour south of San Antonio and about the same distance north of the border city of Laredo.

Cotulla is a beautiful name, calling to mind Ashtabula (which Dylan rhymes with "Honolulu" in the song "You're Gonna Make Me Lonesome When You Go"), a cotillion dance, or Gene Vincent singing "Be-Bop-a-Lula." Originally from Silesia—a region in Central Europe that lies mostly within Poland—the name was brought to this part of South Texas by immigrant Joseph Cotulla in 1868 after he'd served his new country in the Union army.

But I can't think of Cotulla without also thinking about Lyndon Baines Johnson. Because it was Cotulla, and its children, that made a lasting impact on our thirty-sixth president—helping to define him and, by extension, our country.

In 1928, after his freshman year at Southwest Texas State Teachers College, Johnson was hired to teach fifth, sixth, and seventh grades at the Welhausen School in Cotulla—an institution reserved primarily for the Mexican American community. He was soon promoted to be the school's principal (some say because he was the only male teacher on staff) and proceeded to throw himself into both the academic education of the children and what we might today call their social and emotional learning.

Often against great resistance, Johnson pushed the other teachers at Welhausen to do more for, and to expect more from, the children in their care. He organized athletic teams, bought the children volleyballs and softball bats out of his own pocket, and applied his nearly unstoppable determination to helping them improve.

Almost forty years later, as president of the United States, Johnson spoke to a joint session of Congress about his time in Cotulla.

"My students were poor and they often came to class without breakfast, hungry," he said. "They knew even in their youth the pain of prejudice. They never seemed to know why people disliked them. But they knew it was so, because I saw it in their eyes. I often walked home late in the afternoon, after the classes were finished, wishing there was more that I could do. But all I knew was to teach them the little that I knew, hoping that it might help them against the hardships that lay ahead."

Johnson went on to connect his experience in Cotulla with his work on voting rights.

Johnson knew there was nothing inherently lacking in the kids he had taught. They just hadn't had access to the same resources, the same set of expectations, the same investment that gave other kids a leg up.

He also understood that the surest path out of poverty and into opportunity—including the full realization of civil rights—was voting.

Common sense and political experience tell us that elected officials are mostly focused on the people who can either help or hurt their chance of getting reelected. They're typically less concerned about someone who is disenfranchised—either legally or functionally—and therefore unable to vote and affect the outcome of the next election.

As a result, if a neighborhood or community doesn't vote, it's less likely to get the same attention or resources as one that does. And the consequences can be far-reaching. Voter participation rates help determine everything from which schools get the latest technology and facilities to where the city dump is located. (It can also, as we saw in the last chapter, affect whether policies like Medicaid expansion get enacted.)

It's an example of this push-and-pull that exists between representatives and their constituents. And over the years, that dynamic has shaped Texas for better and worse.

Back in Lawrence Nixon's day, El Paso City Council representatives were elected "at large" instead of from distinct geographic districts, meaning there were times when every member of the council was from just one part of town. This was likely intentional. At the time, Black and Mexican American citizens were discouraged or outright banned from voting. Until the mid-1960s, Texas also had a poll tax, which made it even harder for lower-income Texans to vote.

As a result, El Paso and other cities across Texas grew unevenly. The Anglo and wealthier neighborhoods got more resources, better schools, and nicer parks while Mexican American and poorer neighborhoods got landfills, wastewater treatment plants, and underresourced schools. These decisions, in turn, created or closed off opportunities for the people in these neighborhoods and, by extension, for their children and grandchildren. Wealth begat wealth; poverty begat poverty.

When I served on the El Paso City Council, roughly half of the district I represented was in the more affluent and higher-turnout neighborhoods of the west side and Upper Valley. The other half was in the poorer, lower-turnout neighborhoods near downtown and south of the freeway. Though single-member districts had replaced at-large elections in 1979, the effects of the unequal allocation of city resources over the previous century were still obvious. Part of the Modesto Gomez neighborhood south of the freeway, for example, had literally been built on top of a landfill—with homes and parks sinking and rising, and decades-old trash surfacing after heavy rains.

As I fought to direct more resources to areas that were chronically underserved, I'd sometimes get pushback from constituents who lived in neighborhoods north of the freeway. These were people who could afford time off to come to a city council meeting—and who owned their own cars, which made traveling to city hall relatively easy. They also voted at high rates.

On the south side of the freeway, people were much more likely to work a second job, to rely on the bus to get around, and to struggle hard enough to make ends meet that the idea of taking time off and traveling to city hall to advocate for their communities seemed like an unaffordable luxury. Folks on the south side were also less likely to vote, which made it less likely that they'd get the ear of their mayor or city council representative on issues that mattered to them. So historically, that meant that resources went somewhere else, and nothing changed.

To try to break this cycle, I turned to community leaders for help. Pablo Lopez of the South Side Neighborhood Association and Mannys Rodriguez in Chihuahuita were two of my most effective allies—and became key partners as I made the case for their communities to my colleagues on the council. Many of the people in Pablo and Mannys's neighborhood associations couldn't make it to the council meetings or to the weekly town halls that I held. So Pablo and Mannys enabled me to hold dedicated meetings in their neighborhoods, sometimes hosting me in their homes, to guarantee that I would hear from the people I represented—no matter their income or voting history.

Thanks to leaders like Pablo and Mannys, I became a far better representative. And my work took on a level of urgency and accountability that would otherwise have been missing. It resulted in outcomes that helped their neighbors and our city as a whole, including investments in long-deferred street and drainage infrastructure, park renovations, and a new recreation center for a part of El Paso that had long gone without one.

They also gave me hope that we can make government more responsive—because the challenges I saw in El Paso are far from unique.

———

I was in Arlington, outside of Dallas, when I had the chance to meet Alisa Simmons, president of the Arlington NAACP. I could immediately tell Alisa was tough: she wanted to get straight to the point and wasn't interested in formalities or small talk. Alisa's directness was reinforced by a level of profanity that reminded me of my dad—who was the most frequent and creative cusser I'd known.

Alisa's first priority was to make sure I wasn't in Arlington to check a box or get my picture taken with Black leaders. She wanted to make sure I understood what was really happening in her community. She was focused on making big improvements to Arlington, she said, and didn't want to waste any time with anyone who wasn't going to be a serious partner in getting that done.

That day, Alisa told me that her North Texas city—home of the Dallas Cowboys, a Six Flags amusement park, and nearly half a million people—was the largest in the United States without a mass transit system.

"How do people without a car get around?" I asked her.

"They don't," she responded with a colorful expletive thrown in between the two words. She added that some are able to catch rides with friends and family to work or school, and others have been able to use a pilot transit system called Via.

"But what do you do if you need to go to a doctor?" she asked rhetorically. "Or attend your kid's parent-teacher conference? It's hard, almost impossible, for people to get ahead unless they already have wealth in this community. They literally cannot get to where they need to go."

Generations ago, Alisa told me, Arlington city fathers wanted to prevent poor people, who were less likely to own an automobile and more dependent on transit, from moving to or even visiting Arlington. And many of those they kept out were Black.

Alisa also brought my attention to the high number of officer-involved shootings in Arlington. She told me she personally advocated for victims, demanding justice and accountability, no matter the color of their skin. One time, she said, the father of a white woman shot by a police officer in Arlington called her and said, "I saw how you fought for the civil rights of those Black men. I want that for my daughter too."

Today, the work of leaders like Alisa is having an effect.

In 2021, Jim Ross was elected mayor of Arlington. Ross had run on a platform that included improving the anemic transit options available to the community. His victory, and the current popularity of investment in transit, was a turning point. And it might have more than a little to do with the fact that Arlington has become the most diverse city in North Texas. That diversity—in income as well as race and ethnicity—is now being reflected in the electorate and their priorities.

In Arlington that day, Alisa also told me she engages with the city on policing—helping to improve police and community relations. She recognizes that members of law enforcement have one of the toughest, most important jobs anywhere, and it's important to show them respect and support them with the resources and training they need. She also pointed out that we ask police officers to take on too many of the things that we as a society refuse to confront. Whether it's homelessness, mental health access (Texas ranks fiftieth in the nation), or outdated drug control policy (we're one of the last states that forces cops to lock people up for possession of a substance—marijuana—that's legal in most of the rest of the country), we ask police to focus limited resources on issues that could be addressed in other, better ways by elected leaders if only they had the political will to do so. It also comes at the opportunity cost of focusing on deterring, investigating, and solving more violent crime in our communities. But Alisa also made clear that without accountability and the clear expectation that officers will serve and protect everyone equally, public safety suffers and it becomes harder for law enforcement to build and maintain trust in the community.

After years of advocacy and unelected community leadership, Alisa recently decided to run for a seat on the Tarrant County Commissioners Court, which serves Arlington. If she wins, she'll be able to provide more of the leadership on these issues that she has already done so much for.

Meeting with Alisa and talking about the importance of local leadership reminded me of some of the same challenges—like an inadequate transit system—that we faced in El Paso when I first joined the city council.

As in many large cities in Texas, public transit in El Paso has transitioned over the course of the twentieth century from a service everyone used to a service only used by lower-income residents who literally cannot afford a car.

In Lawrence Nixon's day, El Paso had a streetcar system that served the entire city. It was even connected to the transit grid in Ciudad Juárez. Lawyers and janitors, schoolteachers and laborers, the rich and poor, citizens of Mexico and citizens of the United States all rode to work on the same trolleys.

By the time I was growing up, however, all that had changed. Our bus system (then known as Sun City Area Transit, or SCAT) primarily served lower-income workers in El Paso and day laborers, domestic servants, and shoppers from Mexico.

When I was elected to the city council in 2005, decades of disinvestment had left the transit system (whose name had been changed

WE'VE GOT TO TRY

to Sun Metro) in a state of deep disrepair. You couldn't count on the bus to show up on time, or even get you to your destination. Breakdowns were common and the air-conditioning often didn't work. But because Sun Metro customers were most often lower income, and many were permanent legal residents and visa holders, not citizens, they didn't have much sway with the politicians who could actually make a difference.

Chole Galvan wasn't ready to accept that. When I met her early in my time on the council, Chole was already a legend in our Sunset Heights neighborhood. After graduating from Bowie High School in the 1940s, she'd enlisted in the Women's Army Auxiliary Corps and served in World War II. She would proudly tell anyone who would listen that she'd had the chance to sing the national anthem for President Franklin Roosevelt—and would usually belt out some or all of it for you on the spot.

Chole was also a fierce advocate for the people who depend on the bus. She'd invite me to meetings at her home with transit riders, testify at city council hearings, and encourage me to ride specific routes (including the No. 10, which served our neighborhood) so that I could understand exactly what other transit riders were experiencing. Chole would also speak to the press, confront council members in city hall, and generally do whatever it took to get city representatives to pay attention.

Her tenacity paid off and we listened. Thanks to Chole and other advocates like her, the council made significant investments in transit in El Paso—new buses, new dedicated transit lanes, and a new trolley system with refurbished cars from the 1940s. We also set up more rigorous systems of accountability to ensure a much higher level of performance. And I started to hold mobile town hall meetings on the buses to hear directly from the passengers—most of whom were not shy about letting me know where we needed to make improvements.

The advocacy from transit champions like Chole and the focus and the resources from the council paid off. Within four years, El Paso went from being one of the worst places to ride a bus in the country to being one of the best.

———

But while advocacy and civic engagement have produced progress and cause for hope, there is still a lot more to be done.

As usual, most challenges can be traced back to voting rights and the strength of our democracy. When you combine decades of disenfranchisement with redlining, differences in educational opportunity, and an uneven application of the law, you begin to understand the forces driving inequality in Texas. And it's easy to see why some Texans—already facing the toughest voting laws in the country—might be tempted to give up on politics altogether.

But understanding the problem is only half the battle. The other half is figuring out what we're going to do about it.

Progress on voting rights came late to many communities in Texas. Though Johnson's speech to Congress in March 1965 was persuasive—and led to the Voting Rights Act, which he signed into law that summer—it would be another decade before the now-grown Mexican American schoolchildren Johnson taught could fully exercise their right to vote.

The 1975 extension of the Voting Rights Act, signed by President Gerald Ford, finally made it possible for "language minorities"—including Spanish-speaking citizens in Texas—to request voter registration forms and ballots translated into Spanish. That law would also provide the basis for courts to strike down gerrymandered districts that intentionally diluted Latino voting power. And it laid the groundwork for the creation of "opportunity districts" that ensured greater Latino representation in city councils, state legislatures, and Congress. The 1975 VRA extension also proved that voting rights can be a bipartisan issue—with a Republican president extending and enhancing one of the signature achievements of his Democratic predecessor.

But it wouldn't have happened without Barbara Jordan.

The first Black woman elected to Congress from the South, she was acutely conscious of both the opportunities the VRA created and the work that it left unfinished.

"I know firsthand the difficulty minorities have in participating in the political process as equals," she told her colleagues. "The same discriminatory practices which moved the Congress to pass the Voting Rights Act in 1965, and renew it in 1970, are practiced in Texas today."

She became the principal leader of the effort to expand its protections to other targeted groups, including Mexican Americans in her home state of Texas.

"Nearly all the forms of discriminatory voting practices suffered by blacks in the South are being suffered by Mexican Americans in the Southwest," she said.

She had met with and was moved by the men and women who were excluded from participating in elections and holding political power because of their ethnicity and their language—folks like Modesto Rodriguez, who lived in the small town of Pearsall, just thirty miles outside of Cotulla, in Frio County.

A farmer and rancher, Rodriguez found himself squeezed out of economic opportunities by those who held power in Pearsall as soon as he started registering and organizing other Mexican American voters in the community. Loans for his ranch were called and then refinancing denied. Capital dried up for him and anyone else audacious enough to try to upset the status quo.

But as Ari Berman writes in his book *Give Us the Ballot*, the intimidation from the city leaders didn't work as intended. In 1973, Rodriguez and other newly engaged voters in Pearsall helped elect Paul Morales over an Anglo candidate by a margin of sixty-five votes. This, however, was unacceptable to those used to going unchallenged. The sitting county judge ordered an election fraud investigation, exclusively of Mexican American voters, and ultimately overturned the election by throwing out one hundred ballots for being signed with an "X" by those who were illiterate.

And to be sure that power wasn't threatened again, Frio County moved the polling location farther away from Mexican American neighborhoods and then Pearsall annexed nearby Anglo neighborhoods to dilute Mexican American voting strength. They also changed the election hours to make it tougher for farmworkers to find the time to vote at all.

Language was another barrier to voting. Sixty percent of the Spanish speakers in Frio County couldn't read English well enough to understand what was on the ballots. And that's before they had to contend with the gerrymandering.

Because the county redrew the district lines to put 97 percent of Mexican Americans in one district, Anglos were able to control three out of four commissioners' seats, even though the vast majority of the county's population was Mexican American.

This kind of systematic voter intimidation, suppression, and effective disenfranchisement took place across the greater Southwest, even with the Voting Rights Act in place. This led Jordan to take a strong public stand for expanding protections, even though doing so meant going against every single colleague of hers from the Texas congressional delegation, save Congressman Bob Krueger.

But she prevailed upon her other colleagues in the House, worked with like-minded leaders in the Senate, and even overcame a last-minute effort by President Ford to spike the reauthorization.

And so, ten years after Johnson signed the original Voting Rights Act, the extension that Jordan helped spearhead was signed into law.

As Berman writes, "the new VRA made an immediate difference."

The Department of Justice was able to intervene to stop a purge of voters in Texas, and the number of Mexican Americans holding local offices in the state increased dramatically. Civil rights groups and the federal government sued to create fair districts across Texas, and nationally Latinos were elected to city councils, county governments, and the halls of Congress. In 1975 one Mexican American served in Congress. A decade later there would be nine. Today there are fifty-two Hispanic members of Congress.

When I left Congress after my third term in office, I was happy to know that my successor would be Veronica Escobar. A good friend going back to the days when we volunteered together for other candidates and causes in El Paso, Veronica had distinguished herself as an educator, a civic leader, and more recently, as our county judge. I knew that El Paso would be well served by someone who had dedicated so much of her life to public service.

But I was also mindful of the fact that Escobar, along with Sylvia Garcia in Houston, would become the first Mexican American women to represent any community in Congress from the state of Texas. Hard to believe that a state where more than four out of ten residents are Hispanic—a state that has seen so many extraordinarily talented women in other leadership positions—had not elected someone like Veronica long before 2018.

Ensuring that the best leaders can rise to positions of public trust in our country, regardless of race, ethnicity, or gender, was exactly what Barbara Jordan worked for in her career and made possible with the 1975 reauthorization that she led.

While it took far longer than it should have, Escobar's victory gives us hope that we are still able to make progress in ensuring that our government truly reflects the people it purports to represent.

———

When I visited Cotulla a few years back, I thought about Lyndon Johnson and the connection he drew between his experience as an educator and his fight for democracy.

At the time, America and Texas were as divided as I could remember them being, and becoming more polarized by the day. Public school classrooms, I thought, might be the last bastion of democracy and comity in our country.

In most smaller towns like Cotulla, all the schools are public. There isn't the wealth or population to support private education. So whatever your zip code or income, your kids are in the same classroom as everyone else's kids—regardless of political affiliation, religious denomination, or any other difference. Everyone learns together.

And everyone's invested. Literally.

Texas public schools are financed primarily by local property taxes, so everyone in Cotulla pays to educate every child—even after their own kids have grown up and moved away.

School boards in towns like Cotulla are also elected by the public and kept accountable at public board meetings, leading to greater participation, which leads to better outcomes for the kids.

It's why keeping public schools at the center of our communities is so important. Amy and I see this firsthand in the education that our kids—Ulysses, Molly, and Henry—get in El Paso's public schools. It's evident from our conversations with their teachers, the spirit we feel at academic and athletic competitions, and the bonds we make with other parents as we sell hot dogs and nachos for the El Paso High basketball booster club. We go to school board meetings and share our views on issues being voted on. We believe that being involved is good for our kids, and hopefully good for the school and community as well. Public schools strengthen our democracy, and for those schools to be strong we've all got to participate as much as we can.

We also believe that when public schools are starved of resources, when they suffer from low expectations and a general disrespect for the educators who've dedicated their lives to this form of public service, we don't just let our kids down—we imperil the civic life of our community and, by extension, our country.

At a time when some are questioning the value of public education, and educators everywhere feel under attack, we must vigorously make the case for public schools. Like Johnson did in 1928, we need to invest in our classrooms. At a time when the average Texas teacher makes seventy-five hundred dollars per year less than the national average, we need to fully support our educators. And at a time when

Texas invests four thousand dollars per year less than the national average in each student, we need to make sure our young people are getting the support they need to learn and grow.

We also have to listen to the people who are taking on the toughest jobs in some of the most underserved communities—just like President Johnson did. These educators know better than anyone how we can assess progress, determine need, and help spark a lifelong love of learning that will allow all our children to reach their full potential in the classroom.

To help bring a deeply divided and unequal society together, we must make sure public schools are a persuasive choice for families who have other options. And we need to improve the quality of public schools for families who have no other choice. Because better public schools make for a stronger, better democracy.

On that first visit to Cotulla a few years back, I passed a mural depicting a young Lyndon Johnson and the students from the 1928–29 school year at Welhausen. I asked one of the clerks at the courthouse whether anybody who'd been taught by Johnson was still alive. "Not that I know of," the clerk said. "But when Johnson came back in '66 to give his education speech, Pablo Gonzales stood onstage with him. He owns the pharmacy down the street now."

I called Pablo recently and asked him what that moment had been like for him, and what it meant. He told me he first heard President Johnson speak on the radio, when he was a little younger. Johnson, he told me, had said he believed any kid, "even a minority like me," could do anything he set his heart on in America.

It was similar to the sentiment Johnson expressed in his 1965 speech on voting rights, which centered around his experience in Cotulla—

the same speech Dr. King had called "the most moving . . . plea for human rights ever made by any president of this nation."

"I never thought then, in 1928, that I would be standing here in 1965," Johnson declared:

> It never even occurred to me in my fondest dreams that I might have the chance to help the sons and daughters of those students and to help people like them all over this country.
>
> But now I do have that chance, and I'll let you in on a secret—I mean to use it. And I hope that you will use it with me.

Those words flew in the face of Pablo's experiences up to that point. His parents were migrant farmworkers who took Pablo and his sister up north to Wisconsin to pick onions and potatoes in the summer. He remembered *la limpia*, or picking the field clean, with his parents and sister. And he could still picture *la calavera*, a giant tractor that looked like a skull to him, spraying pesticides where the field hands, including the kids, were working.

In the fall, Pablo's family would head back down to Cotulla, a town that had yet to elect anyone who looked like him into a position of prominence. The schools he attended were still functionally segregated and not funded like the schools for the Anglo kids. It reinforced the idea that there was a certain expectation for "Mexicans": primarily field work and other manual labor.

But when he heard Johnson say that he meant to use the full power of the presidency to help the kids of Cotulla reach their full promise, Pablo took it to heart. The most powerful man in the country had promised to help kids like him.

So the following year, when Johnson visited Cotulla to make a speech about the importance of public education, Pablo was there. And as the president of his high school class, he had a chance to shake the hand of the man who had given him hope.

At Welhausen that day, Johnson talked about Pablo and every other kid like him. "For the conscience of America has slept long enough while the children of Mexican Americans have been taught that the end of life is a beet row, a spinach field, or a cotton patch."

He continued:

The citizenship of America today looks forward to the time in the near future when every boy and girl born in this country will have the right and the opportunity to get all the education that they can take.

And when they have that right, when they have that opportunity, from "Head Start" to a college Ph.D. degree, a great many of them will exercise it—they will profit from it—we will have a better and a stronger, and, what is very important, a more prosperous and happier America.

Pablo got his college education at Texas A&I in Kingsville, then qualified for Johnson-era higher education grants matching lower-income minority students with medical profession career tracks. It allowed Pablo to pursue pharmacy at the University of Texas in Austin. After graduation, he worked as a pharmacist in Cotulla and ultimately bought and ran the pharmacy in town.

Pablo took the spirit of Johnson's message and the Voting Rights Act to heart. And like many men and women who had graduated from Welhausen, he became politically involved in ways his parents had not been. Pablo and his classmates joined La Raza Unida, a political party that focused on Mexican American empowerment and pursued a vigorous strategy of voter registration and turnout. Their engagement worked, and one of La Raza's founders, Alfredo Zamora Jr., was elected the first Mexican American mayor of Cotulla in 1970, defeating W. P. Cotulla, a descendant of the city's founding father.

A new political activism and democratic engagement soon swept through the Southwest, with Raza Unida candidates running for local and statewide offices in Texas, Arizona, Colorado, New Mexico, and California. Rosie Castro, mother of future Housing and Urban Development Secretary Julián Castro and Congressman Joaquin Castro, was a founding member of La Raza and nearly won a seat on the San Antonio City Council the year after Zamora was elected in Cotulla.

At the time, the energy and excitement around politics were infectious. "It aroused people to vote," Pablo told me. It also encouraged people to think about running for office. Pablo would serve on the school board and later won election as mayor of Cotulla.

Today, Pablo no longer holds public office. He's also sold the pharmacy, although he still works there. But he's never lost faith in the possibility of this country and what its democracy can achieve. "Every day I pray the rosary," he told me. "I pray for God to bring in justice and to help us work on changing the way things are to what they're supposed to be."

Pablo's story, the story of Cotulla, is the story of American democracy. A future president was able to see himself in the lives of those he taught, and he carried their stories and their struggle with him all the way to the White House. Lyndon Johnson based his fight for voting rights and democracy on the pursuit of justice—seeking to bridge the gap between the way things are and the way they're sup-posed to be. And he took to heart the examples of those whose own fights inspired him—from John Lewis crossing the Edmund Pettus Bridge to the kids of Welhausen in Cotulla trying to cross into a life of dignity and respect.

The Voting Rights Act, the cornerstone of modern American democracy, was born in Cotulla, Texas—when Johnson had the chance to learn from the children he was teaching in the kind of community politicians too often ignore. And it was fully realized through the leadership and example of people like Pablo Gonzales, Alfredo Zamora Jr., and Rosie Castro. These Americans—like so many others—understood that democracy rests on the right to vote. And that right makes everything else possible: including great schools and the ability for every child to reach their full potential as human beings and as American citizens.

6

Fort Bend County

I n July 2018, as a construction team in Sugar Land, Texas, pre-
pared land for a new public school facility, a backhoe operator
noticed what looked like a human bone in the ground.

Construction was immediately halted, and archeologists were
brought in.

The ensuing investigation uncovered something bigger than that
bone in the topsoil: an unmarked burial ground that contained the
remains of ninety-five Black men and boys, aged fourteen to seventy.

These bodies might have been a surprise to the construction team
and the school district that had selected this ground for its new building, but they weren't a surprise to a man named Reginald Moore.

Moore had worked as a prison guard in Fort Bend in the late 1990s.
And the more he learned about the history of the prison at which he

worked and the community in which it was located, the more interested he became in the stories of those who had been locked up there.

He learned that the inmates in his care were incarcerated on the same land as generations of inmates before them, including those who had been imprisoned during the era of convict leasing—a practice that once allowed the state of Texas to essentially "rent out" incarcerated people to farms, ranches, plantations, and construction companies. It also happened to be the same land where enslaved Texans worked right before the end of the Civil War.

Moore drew the connections between the enslaved, the leased, and the currently incarcerated—and saw from the inside that there was deep injustice within the system of justice.

He also came to the conclusion that people so disrespected by society when they were alive were destined to receive no better treatment in death. It was no shock to him, then, that so many had been buried in unmarked graves under the very ground upon which he made his rounds.

———

Even before the Imperial Sugar Company was organized in 1907, Sugar Land was a company town, established in the late nineteenth century on a plantation that had been owned by a Texan man, Colonel Edward H. Cunningham.

After the Civil War, when most of the surrounding sugar plantations went bankrupt for lack of enslaved labor, a couple of growers were able to buy up enough of the faltering operations to build one of the preeminent sugarcane-processing operations in the region. But even as the demand for sugar grew, the ability to harvest cane was limited by the fact that on June 19, 1865, Union soldiers arrived in

Galveston to declare enslaved Texans free. No longer could plantation owners literally buy enslaved laborers to do the backbreaking work that made cane production profitable.

The answer to this sudden shortage in labor was not an increase in wages or greater leverage for prospective workers. Instead, armed with a cynical reading of the Thirteenth Amendment to the U.S. Constitution—which, at the time, forbade both slavery and involuntary servitude *except as a punishment for a crime*—the demand for cheap labor was met by a sharp increase in the arrests of Black men and boys who were then leased to local businesses. This convict leasing system became the financial cornerstone of the Texas criminal justice system following Reconstruction.

Before the Civil War, there were fewer than two hundred people behind bars in all of Texas. After the abolition of slavery, however, the prison population grew exponentially, and the state began leasing prisoners to private companies eager for the cheap labor.

In many ways, this practice continued the forced labor of slavery long after it was technically abolished. And the treatment of the prisoner-laborers was often just as cruel.

Convicts worked "barelegged in wet sugar cane fields, dying like flies in the periodic epidemic of fevers," wrote Bill Mills, one of the prisoners who survived a prison farm known as the Hell Hole on the Brazos.

"The guards often said the men did not cost them any money and the mules did," he wrote, indicating the subhuman working conditions he faced. "That's why there was more sympathy for the mules than for the men."

Whippings were common and the guards were determined to inflict maximum pain, using straps more than five feet long. Prisoners carried the evidence with them for the rest of their lives: their bodies, wrote Mills, were covered in scars "indicating the most reckless and inhuman use of the strap." A visiting doctor wrote that the prisoners' quarters were "in the worst conditions imaginable; the bunks swarmed with vermin."

The punishing conditions in the fields and the abuse from the guards made "a wreck of many strong men in a few years," leaving them disabled and unable to work after release, if they were lucky enough to make it out alive; the annual mortality rate on that farm was 3 percent. When guards killed their prisoners through overwork or extreme punishment, the consequences were minimal, usually resulting in nothing more than a reduction in the usual bonus paid out to them.

The plantation owners who rented out the prisoners would pay state prison guards extra for increasing the number of hours convicts worked in the sugarcane and cotton fields, encouraging them to drive these men to their physical limits and beyond. After all, they didn't care if people died on the job, since they could replace every prisoner they killed by simply arresting someone new.

In short order, the prison laborer system expanded to include more than just men and boys, but also women and girls, both Black and white. Women laborers were spared little abuse, particularly Black women, who were employed in corn and cotton fields, while white women were engaged in domestic labor and "light work."

Huddie William Ledbetter, better known as Lead Belly, was another prisoner-laborer at the Hell Hole on the Brazos, and he darkly commemorated his years there in a version of the song "Midnight Special":

If you're ever down in Houston
Boy, you better walk right

WE'VE GOT TO TRY

And you better not squabble
And you better not fight
Benson Crocker will arrest you
Jimmy Boone will take you down
You can bet your bottom dollar
That you're Sugar Land bound

As stories of abuse escaped the confines of the prison farms, the political will slowly developed to reform the system. A legislative investigation in 1902 revealed troubling levels of both escapes and deaths at the work farms. It emerged that, due to unrelenting labor, unsanitary conditions, and the likelihood of being shot by guards, entering the convict leasing system in Fort Bend decreased a prisoner's life expectancy by seven years.

But evil as it may have been, it remained hugely profitable—both for the plantation owners and for the state. Just one of Fort Bend's prison farms, the Harlem State Farm, netted the Texas government more than $230,000 from the 165 African American prisoners it leased out in 1892, which is equivalent to over $7 million today.

The investigative committee recommended abolishing convict leasing altogether, but they found no support from the rest of the legislature or the governor. Their work was ignored, and then dismissed. Absent any serious checks on greed, the convict leasing system continued.

Luckily for the prisoners in Fort Bend, there was eventually one thing even more powerful than the plantation owners' profits: legislators' fear of losing their reelections.

In 1908, six years after the investigation, a distraught prison chaplain at Huntsville decided that if the cruel treatment of the convicts wasn't compelling enough for the legislature to implement changes, then he would try and get the story directly to the people—and voters—of Texas.

The chaplain shared his eyewitness accounts with a young reporter from the *San Antonio Express* named George Waverley Briggs, who followed up with his own investigation and was soon able to publish a series of sensational stories that documented the brutal reality of convict leasing for a much broader readership. The horrifying details about the uncontrolled and arbitrary whippings, the shooting of prisoners, and the desperation of the convicts were read widely across the state.

Briggs profiled one prisoner who had chopped off two of his own fingers in order to escape a work camp, only to be beaten unconscious by his guards for doing so. In another story, Briggs described some of the creative ways in which men on the work farms were punished, including being thrown on anthills and dragged behind horses.

He also documented the miserable conditions under which women labored:

On the women's farm, a year ago last spring, a child was born in the field sans attention, medical care or decency. Hours afterward, according to the statement of a witness, the sand of the cotton field still adhered to and lacerated its tender little body, as it writhed in the first activities of life. . . .

On the morning of the child's birth the prison mates of the mother protested against her being sent to the field. Courageous from the maternal instinct that lives even in the breast of convicts they braved the discipline of the prison regime and sought to dissuade the assistant in charge of them from his indicated course. Their protestation availed nothing. The woman was ordered to the field to hoe her row with her companions.

By writing these stories for mass consumption, Briggs was able to succeed where the investigative committee had failed: awakening the conscience of the electorate and generating the popular will to do something about it.

The resulting public pressure forced the state legislature and governor to once again take up the issue of prison reform. This time, they were armed with the knowledge that public sentiment was fully engaged and would help hold lawmakers accountable for enacting real changes.

A "Penitentiary Investigating Committee," comprised of state senate and state house members, was formed, and they personally investigated conditions inside the prison walls and out on the work farms in places like Sugar Land and Fort Bend. Just like the 1902 committee, they encountered a system of brutality that had metastasized under the willful neglect of regulators and lawmakers. But unlike their predecessors, they knew that their next steps would be imminently judged by the voters in their districts who had read Briggs's graphic accounts of the convict leasing system. In short, they actually had to do something about it.

After consolidating their findings, the legislators made their recommendation to the governor in simple terms: "We recommend that the contract and labor share farm system be abolished not later than January 1, 1912." This time, the recommendation was quickly accepted. And the convict leasing system, which had, to date, claimed an estimated thirty-five hundred lives and irreparably damaged thousands more, finally came to an end.

Democracy in Texas, though it remained deeply flawed, had, in this case, prevailed over the extraordinary cruelty and reckless profiteering of the convict leasing system.

This is a reminder that, just as with the success of voting rights in 1965, a deeply unequal democracy—one that in both instances had disenfranchised African Americans—can still achieve important outcomes. In both these cases it happened by building public pressure with the help of a free and independent press, pressure that galvanized Anglo voters to push their elected representatives to act on issues of deep injustice. That these injustices were borne overwhelmingly by African American citizens who were denied the right to vote makes it all the more remarkable. The broadcasts of the brutality of Bloody Sunday in 1965 and the news stories of the Hell Hole on the Brazos in 1908 demonstrate that far from being the "enemy of the people," a free press is fundamental to the functioning of our democracy.

But if convict leasing's abolition is a story of what happens when the institutions of democracy, including a free press, start to work, then the reason that convict leasing existed in the first place is a story of what happens when a democracy dies.

———

The question remains: How did such a gross miscarriage of justice take place in Fort Bend County, anyway?

After the Civil War, Fort Bend made one of the more successful transitions to democracy of any county of the former Confederacy.

At one point in the mid-1880s, just two decades after the Civil War ended, more than half the elected offices in Fort Bend County were held by Black citizens. In fact, the first Black sheriff elected anywhere in the United States was Fort Bend County's Walter Moses Burton, in 1869.

But as Reconstruction ended in the 1870s and federal protection for voting rights was withdrawn, this success was violently overturned.

Though economic and social power was still firmly controlled by Anglos—the vast majority of wealth was in white hands and Fort Bend schools remained firmly segregated—many white leaders felt so threatened by the small pockets of Black political power that they organized to end it.

By the summer of 1888, a group of young white Fort Bend men, resentful of Reconstruction and the phenomenal Black political success their county had witnessed over the past fifteen years, organized the "Jaybird" preliminary primary—essentially a primary before the Democratic primary, not unlike the one conducted by the People's Party in Washington County. This functioned as a whites-only filter for candidates in local elections and began the transformation of a successful local multiracial democracy into full political apartheid.

The Jaybirds were opposed in their efforts by the Woodpeckers, a group largely comprised of Republican Unionists. During that year's political contests, the Jaybirds' provocations and threats became so disruptive that the Texas Rangers were forced to supervise the elections, which were handily and lawfully won by Woodpecker candidates, both Black and white.

But the tension between the groups continued to escalate. In early 1889, with animus rising in the wake of the previous year's election, the Woodpecker and pro-Reconstruction tax assessor, Kyle Terry, killed a Jaybird leader.

In a testament to how quickly political and even racial sentiment can change, it was Terry's father, Benjamin Franklin Terry, who had organized the Eighth Texas Cavalry Regiment for the Confederate States of America in 1861. Within a generation, the younger Terry had become a supporter of Black political participation—willing, in fact, to die for it.

Within a year, Kyle Terry would be shot dead, as he approached the courthouse in Galveston to take the stand in his murder trial. The son of the martyred Confederate hero was himself martyred as he fought against the Confederate resurgence in Fort Bend.

The violent feud continued throughout 1889, with Jaybirds and Woodpeckers targeting each other for beatings and assassinations. It culminated in a pitched battle outside the county courthouse during which the Fort Bend sheriff, a Woodpecker, was killed. The white supremacist Jaybirds won the battle and, with the complicity of the state government, were able to dictate the terms of the peace.

The resulting settlement ended up replacing every single Woodpecker elected official with a Jaybird, effectively overturning the results of the 1888 election, sanctioning the violent overthrow of numerous democratically elected officials, and effectively ending multiracial democracy in Fort Bend County for more than sixty years. (The Jaybird primary would not be outlawed until 1953.)

Of course, the officially sanctioned Jaybird whites-only primary had a significance far beyond Fort Bend. It would also serve as the blueprint for the statewide whites-only primary that Lawrence Nixon would encounter more than thirty years later.

And the other consequences weren't only political.

It was the erosion of democracy in Fort Bend that allowed for the full realization of convict leasing—slavery by another name.

The county that had elected the first Black sheriff in American history now had a Jaybird sheriff who would arrest Black men and boys to satisfy the workforce needs of local companies and plantations. With no representation in political office, with the reins of government firmly in the hands of white supremacists, with the federal government in full retreat from protecting their constitutional rights, African Americans were defenseless against this injustice and paid the price.

———

The construction team that uncovered the bodies of the ninety-five men and boys in Sugar Land in 2018 had also unearthed the history and the truth that Reginald Moore had pursued for much of his adult life.

For nearly twenty years prior to the 2018 discovery, Moore had sought justice for the unremembered people who had built the economic success of the community where he now lived. At its height, the convict leasing system was so widespread throughout Texas that even the state capitol was built by convict laborers.

He wanted their graves found and marked, and he pushed elected leaders, prison officials, and others to invest the time and resources to make it possible. He wanted to make sure that their contributions were remembered, their legacy honored, and that some justice was done now, given the grave injustice done to them in the past.

When it turned out that the bodies discovered by the school district in Fort Bend in 2018 were those of Black convict laborers, arrested for the convenience of local industry on charges of vagrancy, loitering, and other minor as well as made-up crimes, it was, among other things, a clear validation of what Reginald Moore had been saying all along.

The investigation of the remains revealed that some of the men and boys had literally been worked to death. Their skeletons displayed evidence that muscles had been torn free of the bones. The dead had been buried without ceremony, and new Black bodies were arrested to replace them.

Moore, however, wasn't only concerned with this gruesome past.

He knew, as a Black man, that while this country might promise equal protection under the law, it was far from delivering it.

Not long after the Sugar Land discovery, the entire country was forced to acknowledge the injustice that Moore had long worked to overcome when George Floyd was publicly murdered by a Minneapolis police officer.

But Floyd and Moore had a connection that extended beyond that moment. Before moving to Minnesota, Floyd had grown up in the same community as Moore, had attended the same high school in Houston's Third Ward, and had been raised in the same segregated system of justice. Well before his murder at the hands of a Minneapolis police officer, Floyd bore the consequences of the gulf between the promise and practice of equal treatment under the law in Texas—something Moore had been calling attention to for decades.

Moore also understood that, while the convict leasing program ended in 1912, the idea of privatizing public justice did not. In fact, seventy-three years later, Texas became the first state to turn back to private prisons to actively *expand* its incarceration capacity. Today, Texas holds more of its own people in prisons run by corporations than any other state in America.

Nor did public pressure to end the inhumane treatment of prisoners in the convict leasing program a century ago address all of the systems of injustice within the criminal justice system—many of which continue to this day.

Those connections—between slavery and convict leasing and between the loss of voting rights and the loss of justice—that determined the future and fate of Fort Bend were not obvious to many until Reginald Moore stepped up to make them.

Moore understood the nature of doing time in Texas prisons. But for those who don't know, the facts are sobering. As was the case a hundred years ago, those behind bars tend to be people of color, primarily Black and Latino. And though they are not worked to death, their opportunities and options in life after release are severely constrained. (The requirement to check a box on every employment application form indicating a prior felony and the likelihood of being disqualified for a student loan are but two examples.) The incarceration rate for whites in Texas is 768 per 100,000; for Blacks it is 2,855 per 100,000.

Overall, the state of Texas locks up a higher percentage of its residents than almost any democracy on earth.

This has produced a direct threat to Texas democracy itself. With nearly half a million Texans on probation or parole and another quarter million behind bars at any given time, Texas is locking up over seven hundred thousand potential voters, all of whom are ineligible to cast a ballot until they are off paper, meaning that they have satisfied all the conditions of their probation, as well as other requirements from the court.

Furthermore, there are hundreds of thousands more Texans who are currently out of prison *and* off paper, who may nevertheless be unaware that they have the right to register to vote. And then there are those who may know that they are eligible to vote, but who have no interest in interacting with government or law enforcement again. When you add them all up, that is simply far too many disenfranchised Texans, whose voices are not heard by our elected officials. And the consequences of these policies can be dire.

Consider the story of Crystal Mason. While still on supervised release for a federal tax fraud conviction in 2016, she attempted to vote in that year's presidential election in Tarrant County.

Her vote was cast as a "provisional ballot," because the poll judge could not find her name on the rolls. She later told authorities that she did not know she was ineligible, was not informed beforehand, and never would have attempted to vote if she had been made aware of that rule. The last thing she wanted to do was risk her freedom once again.

Though her provisional vote was never counted—the entire purpose of a provisional ballot is to let people whose registration is in question record their choice, and then allow election officials to later judge whether to count it—she was tried and convicted of the state felony of voting illegally and sentenced to five years in prison. For trying to vote. She is appealing her conviction today, but the intended message to prospective voters who have had a brush with the criminal justice system in Texas is loud and clear: better not to try.

But amid all this infuriating and senseless injustice within our democracy, there are still strong signs of hope, and cause for cautious optimism.

The same year that those ninety-five bodies were uncovered in Sugar Land, a man by the name of KP George was elected county judge—an executive position akin to mayor—becoming the first person of color to hold that position in Fort Bend County history.

George was born in a small village in India. He didn't own a pair of shoes until he was in fourth grade, and he didn't learn English until he was an adult. He came to the United States in the early 1990s and moved to Sugar Land in 1999. There he started a small business, ran for and won an election to serve on the local school board, and now presides over one of the nation's fastest-growing counties—and one of its most diverse.

I asked Judge George what he made of the transformation in Fort Bend: from the county whose all-white Jaybird primary hadn't been struck down until 1953 and was once home to one of the most brutal convict-leasing arrangements in the country to the county that had now elected a man of color to its top political position.

"It's more than what it means to me. It's what it means to the people," he said. "Now we have representation. Now the judge's office is open to all the people. We are looking at issues of access and correcting disparities in the county. We want to level the playing field and make sure that everyone truly has the opportunity to succeed. Everyone."

He went on to tell me about how access to the ballot and political success have brought about policy changes that are driving small business growth and job creation: a nationally renowned small business grant program, a summer jobs program for young people, and a more efficient business permits program. The county has also initiated a large-scale study to ensure that county contracts are awarded more fairly going forward.

And what about people like Reginald Moore, I asked him, who tirelessly fought for justice for fellow county residents, including those who had long been dead? Judge George sees him as a hero who wasn't recognized in his own time, but whose struggle contributed to the diversity, justice, and success that Fort Bend is beginning to see today.

"He was a lone fighter," George said. "People laughed at him, mocked him. He would plead for justice at these school board meetings and city council meetings, and they thought he was just wasting their time. But he never gave up, even when he was all alone." George paused. "Sometimes we will not see the fruit of our fight, but the fight will go on."

In other words, his fight was a long and lonely one, but it mattered that he tried. His was the same spirit as Lawrence Nixon's.

Reginald Moore died in 2020. But his fight did not end there.

The community took up his cause and began raising funds for a new memorial recognizing what had been done to the "Sugar Land 95." Samuel Collins, who traveled and worked with Moore before his death, told the *Houston Chronicle,* "It's not that we want to live in the past or that we want to be victims. What we want is the truth to be told so we can learn from it and never repeat the mistakes of the past."

In 2020, two years after Judge George's victory, Eric Fagan was elected sheriff of Fort Bend County, becoming the first African American elected to that position since Walter Moses Burton won the post in 1869. He defied all odds to become the top law enforcement official in a county that had, not too long ago, been infamous for targeting its own Black citizens.

"I was raised by my mom in a low-income area," he told one reporter, just a few months after he was sworn in. "Statistically I should be in prison."

And that same year, Bridgette Smith-Lawson became the first African American elected as Fort Bend County attorney. In 2021, she watched the Jaybird Monument, a symbol that had long stood in the county seat, come down.

"Fort Bend is the most diverse county in this country," she said at the time. "This artifact did not in my opinion have any place in the current climate and environment."

None of these steps forward can erase the shameful history of racism and incarceration in Fort Bend. But they do show that progress through the democratic process *is* possible—as long as we never stop fighting for it.

After all, the heroes who ushered in the revival of democracy in Fort Bend have produced something that is beginning to look a lot like justice.

7

The Border, Part I

There is a place along the Rio Grande on the Texas side of the international border whose name means "what lies ahead." It's quiet enough that you can hear the sounds of the river and the wildlife that is drawn to it, unlike other border communities where the noise of industry and the bustle of human activity can drown it out. This makes it almost hard to imagine it before, to picture Porvenir as anything but the ghost town it is today—to see how this place was once home to a vibrant community.

The end of that once vibrant community came on January 28, 1918. Early that morning, Texas Rangers, with support from the U.S. Army's Eighth Cavalry Regiment, joined local ranchers in a door-to-door roundup of the men and boys of Porvenir, Texas. At the time, the town had the misfortune of being one of the closest Mexican American communities to a ranch that had been raided the month before by men believed to be partisans of Mexican general Pancho Villa.

The ranchers, Rangers, and soldiers captured fifteen men and boys from the village, the youngest only sixteen, and marched them into the desert, where they were lined up and shot dead.

Juan Flores, who was twelve at the time, was one of the first to encounter the killing field. The men had been shot so many times, and from such close range, that as he examined the mangled bodies—including his father's—he assumed they'd been chopped up with machetes.

Though the Rangers tried to cover up the massacre by claiming there had been a shootout, the Texas Legislature's lone Mexican American member, José Tomás Canales, insisted on a full investigation. Only after the witnesses were heard and the evidence collected was the captain of the Rangers company forced to admit that he had led an organized execution of defenseless men and boys—and not the armed bandits he'd claimed they were.

The cover-up was exposed and the survivors were able to tell their stories thanks to Representative Canales. But there would be no real accountability or justice in the end: not one Ranger or soldier involved with the massacre—the largest slaughter of Mexican Americans in our country's history for over one hundred years—was ever charged. The captain behind the massacre would go on to have a long career with the Rangers.

Meanwhile, most of Porvenir's residents would flee to Mexico, and the town would soon cease to exist—literally wiped off the map.

But it would not be forgotten.

————

I was born and raised in El Paso, another border city, up the river from Porvenir.

El Paso and its sister city of Ciudad Juárez are unlike any other place in the world. Nearly three million people share this Chihuahuan Desert valley carved into the southern Rocky Mountains by the Rio Grande.

You'll have a hard time finding another two cities in two countries conjoined in this way: our street grids interconnected, our families interrelated, our economies interdependent. While we may be isolated from the centers of power and influence in our respective countries, we have each other. Two languages, two cultures, two nationalities. One people.

It's also breathtakingly beautiful, physically and culturally. Rising more than four thousand feet from the desert floor, the twin cities are nestled between the river and the surrounding mountains, which, while studded with cactus, mesquite, and desert shrubs, are unadorned by the carpet of grasses or the canopy of trees that dominate other parts of the Rockies.

The Franklin Mountains run right down the middle of El Paso, with the river, the freeway, and the city's neighborhoods wrapping around them. There's a road that skirts the high edge of the southern end of the Franklins from which you can look out over the valley. From that perspective, El Paso and Juárez are indistinguishable.

There is a mural in South El Paso by the artists known as Los Dos that depicts the two cities as conjoined twin sisters whose powerful gazes greet travelers as they come north across one of the international bridges that join El Paso and Juárez. There's always been a strong connection between these cities—geographic, familial, and cultural.

Our identity is fused in other ways as well. While English and Spanish are spoken on both sides of the border, there are phrases, words, and inflections that combine the two tongues in ways that you don't hear outside of the borderlands. You'll notice it as people mingle under the stars before the mariachis begin playing when you take your family out to the Chamizal, an international park and amphitheater that commemorates the successful negotiation of a land dispute between the two countries in the 1960s.

Many of the kids I went to school with at Mesita Elementary led their lives on both sides of the border. Their parents might have a home in El Paso, but they'd spend the weekends with their grandparents in Juárez. When they'd cross back over on Monday morning, they'd join thousands of other cross-border travelers on our international bridges: U.S.-based plant managers crossing south to run the maquilas of multinational corporations on the Mexican side; Mexican-based college students crossing north to attend the University of Texas at El Paso, which offers in-state tuition for residents of Juárez; and a multitude of other *fronterizos*—shoppers, day laborers, tourists, and people just crossing to visit family, go to a movie, or have a drink at a bar on the other side.

But what was normal for me and the people of this community was seen as dangerous to so much of the rest of the country. That disconnect between the beauty and opportunity I know from growing up on the border and the fear and panic that it can present in the popular imagination creates an opening into which comes the evil of the Porvenir massacre from a hundred years ago—or a more recent slaughter of border residents much closer to home.

The border is so physically isolated and removed from the centers of power and popular culture in the United States and Mexico that it ends up being defined by those who've never been there, whose imaginations run wild with danger.

It's not just in the movies and popular culture. It reverberates in political speech, in the halls of Congress, in the sensational news coverage and punditry, and in the legislation and policies that flow from the opinion makers and lawmakers who feed off one another's fear and who see profit and political opportunity in casting the border as lawless wasteland. But this isn't new. It's a story that goes back to 1848, when the border was created, and continues through to this moment.

Never mind that U.S. border communities are far safer than the rest of the country. Or that millions of American jobs depend on the binational manufacturing, trade, and logistics hubs of Juárez/El Paso, Nuevo Laredo/Laredo, and Tijuana/San Diego.

Now, this is not to say that there aren't real challenges at the border. There are. And we must guard against and do our best to stop the very real threats of human smuggling and illegal drug trafficking. But the answer to these challenges isn't to demonize the border and all who cross over it.

So why does it happen? And why do so many of our leaders treat immigration as an obstacle, rather than an opportunity, for our country?

It might be because the border is where we meet the rest of the non-Anglo world, where we are connected to people who don't speak English, who are economically far poorer than we are, who don't have the institutions and traditions that we take for granted. This can be made to seem frightening and alien, especially if those in power warn of "invasions" or "infestations" of brown-skinned people, even referring to them as "animals."

While this dynamic has always existed, there have been moments that have made it worse.

The terror attacks that killed thousands of Americans in New York, Washington, D.C., and Pennsylvania on September 11, 2001, was one of them.

Those attacks, perpetrated by foreign nationals here on non-immigrant visas, unleashed an extraordinary focus on foreigners inside our country and at our borders. Our worst fears about what the rest of the world could do to us had been realized, producing a panic that upended our approach to immigration and the border. Despite the fact that all of the 9/11 hijackers were from the Middle East and North Africa and successfully entered the United States at major metropolitan airports, the U.S.-Mexico border witnessed a militarized buildup of walls, sensors, drones, aerostat blimps, and Border Patrol agents.

It's as though an injury to one part of our body politic produced an outsized autoimmune response throughout the rest of the system. While our post-9/11 policies might have reduced our susceptibility to a specific kind of threat, they came at a terrible price, especially for those on the border.

The response led to wars that we are just now ending. It led to the creation of massive surveillance programs that continue to this day. It made our society more guarded, requiring us, for example, to take our shoes and belts off before we board an airplane. And it also hastened the militarization of our border, causing an explosion in U.S.-Mexico border security spending.

Since 9/11, federal spending on immigration enforcement has increased from $4.3 billion to $25 billion a year, eclipsing spending on other principal federal law enforcement agencies like the FBI and the DEA. All told, we have spent more than $315 billion on immigration enforcement since 9/11 and have tripled the number of people working on it.

We've tasked the men and women who serve in the Border Patrol and in Customs with everything from intercepting human traffickers to stopping the smuggling of illegal drugs like fentanyl to remaining vigilant against other possible threats to our country and our border communities. They play an essential role in keeping our country safe.

But the massive spending increase and ginned-up anxiety about the border have also led to boondoggles—like a billion-dollar border sensor system that never worked and that ended up producing no additional security gains.

The rise of border walls and a more militarized approach to border security (under both Republican and Democratic administrations) have also pushed migrants into far more treacherous terrain. In 2021 alone, U.S. Customs and Border Protection reported that 567 people died trying to cross into the United States.

Though we've dramatically increased our capacity for interdiction and incarceration, we have not in any meaningful way reduced the number of people trying to come to the United States. In 2002, the year that the Department of Homeland Security was created, there were approximately 955,000 apprehensions of undocumented immigrants. In 2019, there were 977,500.

While immigration numbers have waxed and waned since 9/11, two decades later, we are seeing some of the highest levels of crossing attempts into the United States.

That's because we have failed to do anything about the underlying issues that produce this dynamic in the first place. People don't make the decision to come to this country based on how many miles of wall they face, or the number of Border Patrol agents, or the quantity of detention beds, or whether their asylum claim will be adjudicated in a timely fashion. In fact, many come because they have no other choice.

Following devastating climate disasters in the Caribbean and Central America over the last decade; civil wars and political instability in those same regions over the last seventy years; and an insatiable demand for illegal drugs in the United States that has created crippling pressure on the legal and political institutions in the countries from which these drugs originate and through which they transit, we are witnessing unprecedented migration from places like Haiti, El Salvador, Honduras, Guatemala, and Mexico.

And because the last major rewrite of our immigration laws took place in 1986, we don't have the legal and administrative structure to deal with the changing dynamics of immigration to the United States. All of this has produced a chaotic and disorderly system of immigration that provides incentives for people on both sides to evade laws that in no way match the conditions, demands, and values of our country in the twenty-first century.

If, for example, you live in Mexico and want to join your sister who is a naturalized citizen in America, your wait time for a family-based green card could be nearly two decades. If you own a farm in the Panhandle and want to sponsor an immigrant worker, it could take thousands of dollars to hire just one person for the summer months.

If you are an asylum seeker fleeing gang violence in Guatemala, your asylum request may take years to resolve and, thanks to the Orwellian-named Migrant Protection Protocol, you will be forced to wait on the south side of the U.S.-Mexico border—in a shelter or on the streets—while your request is adjudicated. And if you came here to earn money and then return to your home country, the problems with our limited guest worker programs and our increasingly militarized border might cause you to instead stay and try to bring your family here, so that you don't have to risk crossing the border again.

We unfairly put the onus of managing this broken system on Border Patrol agents, forcing them to do what no one should be asked to. In addition to stopping and apprehending drug smugglers and human traffickers, these are the men and women who encounter stranded children and desperate families who are on the verge of death after surviving a harrowing two-thousand-mile journey to our country. And they are the ones who find the bodies when those immigrants and asylum seekers don't survive.

They, along with Catholic charities like El Paso's Annunciation House and other nonprofits that provide shelter, food, medicine, and travel support for refugees and asylum seekers in border communities, are the ones tasked with holding what passes for an immigration system together. And we owe them, and the rest of our country, something much better.

Until we change our immigration laws to reflect current demands and challenges—like increasing the per-country immigration caps, speeding up the adjudication of visa requests and asylum claims, and implementing a viable guest worker program—we will continue to create incentives for people to break the law and place federal law enforcement and border communities in this untenable position.

And unless we are serious about addressing the factors that cause people to leave their home countries in the first place—including confronting our contribution to climate change, the illegal drug trade, and political and economic instability throughout the Western Hemisphere—we will continue to see people show up at our border in increasing numbers for the foreseeable future. No surge in Border Patrol staffing, no amount of wall construction, no level of clampdown on border communities will stop that.

Absent real fundamental change, we will only see more of the same: desperate people taking desperate measures to flee desperation in their home countries; overstretched social service agencies and immigration courts; reactionary rhetoric that inflames more than it illuminates; and a metastasized response that prioritizes interdiction and incarceration over long-term solutions.

Why is all of this in a book about democracy?

Because when we fail to seriously address a problem as big as this one; when we choose stopgaps to help us in the short term at the expense of the real work and decision-making necessary to solve the underlying challenge over the long term; when we're not honest with ourselves and our fellow Americans about what is happening and why it is happening, we open the door to the charlatans and demagogues who stoke anxiety and fear about immigrants to further their own political ambitions.

You get ideas like the Muslim travel ban. Family separation. Kids in cages.

It becomes easier and more popular to scapegoat immigrants for problems with crime, or jobs, or social services.

Or even elections.

Just look at how former president Trump relied on the old standby of a frightening "other" to blame for his electoral shortcomings. In 2016, he lost the popular vote to Hillary Clinton by nearly three million votes, but he blamed that loss on "illegal immigrants" who he claimed voted in record numbers. (They didn't.)

Those lies were quickly echoed by a growing network of supporters and media enablers. Before long, the idea that undocumented immigrants were voting at staggering, threatening levels was pursued by the elections officials responsible for overseeing the security of the vote in states like North Carolina, Kansas, Colorado, Florida, and Texas. Though Trump's claims were disproven, the truth did little to dampen the drive to blame immigrants for certain political outcomes or to scare Americans about the specter of undocumented immigrants overtaking the rest of the electorate.

Here in Texas, we saw Trump's allegations adopted, echoed, and weaponized with startling efficiency. The secretary of state alleged that there were likely tens of thousands of voters who were illegally on the rolls. Trump in turn amplified the claim on Twitter, even though it was false.

And long after the 2020 election was decided, when Trump was espousing new election lies—that illegal votes came not just from immigrants but via the mail—Governor Greg Abbott audited the results of four key Texas counties, again on the false claim that there was widespread voter fraud.

Not to be outdone, Senator Ted Cruz based his opposition to a proposed federal voting rights bill on the baseless claim that it would "register millions of illegal aliens to vote." Tapping into that same deep reservoir of nativist fear of a takeover or replacement by immigrants, Cruz said the bill would "dilute the votes of American citizens."

And while all of this was going on, the Texas attorney general's voter fraud unit spent $2.2 million of taxpayers' money to publicly prosecute this supposed fraud. And out of seventeen million registered voters, they found three cases of minor fraud. Hardly a crisis of voter integrity.

Nonetheless, the Texas state legislature used that same unfounded fear to push through the most restrictive elections bill in the country. When Governor Abbott signed it into law in 2021, he made it harder to vote in Texas than in any other state.

———

This accelerating attack on the right to vote is alarming but is not out of rhyme with what has come before.

For much of American history, those in power have used fear—of fraud, of scarcity, of "the other"—to justify voting restrictions against Americans they could easily demonize and scapegoat. One hundred and fifty years ago, it was the Irish, two million of them, fleeing famine and widespread death, who showed up at our maritime borders seeking refuge and legal status in America. Their cultural and religious differences and extreme poverty provoked anxiety that they would use elections and the right to the vote to overwhelm the status quo.

That is, until they became more integrated into the fabric of American life. Just a couple of decades after peak Irish immigration, Cork-born labor leader Denis Kearney would end his fiery speeches to thousands outside San Francisco City Hall by demanding that "whatever happens, the Chinese must go!"

In the years after Lawrence Nixon came to El Paso in 1910—the years of the Mexican Revolution—politicians and the press in the border community profited by stoking fears of Mexicans. El Pasoans were told that their neighbors to the south would bring illegal voting, crime, disease, and drugs.

Political paranoia led to paranoid policies. In 1915, El Paso became the first city in the country to outlaw marijuana, following sensational news stories of Mexicans who developed a "lust for human blood" and killed innocent Americans while high on cannabis.

But it was bigger than the changes made to the criminal justice system. A wave of political terror against Mexicans and Mexican Americans was unleashed throughout the borderlands.

Between 1910 and 1920, cheered on by other politicians and members of the press, local vigilantes, at times with the complicity of law enforcement in Texas, took the law into their own hands—and took the lives of thousands of Mexican Americans and Mexican citizens. One editorialist wrote in the *Laredo Times*, "There is a serious surplus population there that needs eliminating."

Texans of Mexican heritage were shot, hanged, burned alive, or beaten to death. At times, attempts were made to justify the brutality as a response to the chaos and uncertainty of the ongoing Mexican Revolution. Violence between factions and toward U.S-owned interests in Mexico led to fears among many Anglos in the U.S. that Texans of Mexican descent might be radicalized by the war.

For some, these fears were confirmed when Mexican-based *sediciosos*, or secessionists, began sporadically raiding Anglo ranches from across the border. In 1915, the incendiary Plan de San Diego was published by unknown authors, calling for an uprising against Anglo rule in South Texas and the murder of all Anglo men older than sixteen. Following its publication, there were more than two dozen raids that resulted in twenty-one Anglo American deaths. It's clear that Mexicans and Mexican Americans were not simply victims of a whites-only purge; there was a real, if small, insurgent movement and an effort to secure, through force of arms, the political power that had been usurped by Anglos along the border and in South Texas.

But the response to the raids and violence connected to the plan was far greater than the threat posed by the Mexican separatists. Border violence empowered Anglo ranchers and state law enforcement to dispense a wild, violent justice against Mexican nationals, Mexican Americans, and Tejanos (descendants of the original Spanish settlers).

It also provided the perfect opportunity to reduce the political power and civil rights of Hispanic Texans. Nine months after the Plan de San Diego was revealed, prominent Tejanos Jesús Bazán and Antonio Longoria reported the theft of horses on their ranch in Hidalgo County to a unit of Texas Rangers who were encamped close by. Instead of helping, the Rangers shot the men in the back and left them to die on the side of the road, warning residents not to move or bury their bodies.

Despite the prominence of the victims—including Longoria, who had been a Hidalgo County elections official—and despite the public nature of the execution, no investigation was conducted, no death certificates were issued, and no one was ever prosecuted for the murders.

The impunity with which Mexican Americans and Tejanos could be terrorized and killed drove many out of their communities and left their property susceptible to forfeiture. It significantly reduced economic and political power for families that had in some cases lived in the borderlands for generations. And it helped lead to a massacre like the one in Porvenir.

This violence changed the dynamics of power in border commu-

WE'VE GOT TO TRY

nities. Counties that saw extrajudicial executions also saw a decrease in their Mexican American populations, even as the overall number of immigrants from Mexico increased throughout Texas. These same counties are now among the poorest, with some of the lowest levels of voter participation, in the state.

The terrorists' focus on political power is not incidental. Without recourse to law enforcement, the courts, and elected office, Texans of Mexican descent on the border no longer had as much say in the destiny of the state. After Canales left the legislature in 1920, there would not be another Latino elected to the statehouse for thirty-five years.

After the United States entered World War I, Texas created a new branch of state law enforcement: the "Loyalty Rangers," who were tasked with rooting out anti-American behavior. Largely, they focused their efforts on the political participation of Texans of Mexican descent, never mind the loyal and patriotic example set by Mexican immigrants who enlisted in the U.S. Army during the war.

In the 1918 elections in the South Texas city of Alice, total votes cast declined from three hundred in the primary to only sixty-five in the general election. One political observer noted, "The former large number of Mexicans who have voted in previous elections was conspicuous by their absence." No longer did they "[congregate] at the polls." Instead, they gathered uptown, "[discussing] among themselves this new thing of being watched by the Rangers."

Much of this violence and political intimidation was uncovered in the Canales hearings that investigated the Porvenir massacre. Canales weathered the contempt of his colleagues and threats on his life in order to produce nearly fifteen hundred pages of documentary evidence on the Rangers. Though he was unsuccessful at winning full accountability for the crimes committed, his work resulted in the disbandment of the Loyalty Rangers and greater oversight of the regular Rangers.

His great-nephew Terry Canales represents part of the Rio Grande Valley in the state legislature today. "What J.T. [Canales] did took guts," he told me. "He was ridiculed and looked down upon by the leadership in the legislature. The committee chairmen would try to humiliate him by saying, 'The Chair recognizes the greaser from the border' or 'the spic from Brownsville.' And some of the Rangers threatened to kill him, to the point that he had a bodyguard of other House members escorting him into and out of the hearings. What he uncovered was so gruesome and damaging to the status quo in Texas that the transcripts were not released for more than fifty years."

State Representative Sam Ealy Johnson was one of those who accompanied Canales as his bodyguard, ensuring the safety of the man who sought to expose violent voter suppression.

And it wouldn't be the only time that a member of the Johnson family stepped up to protect the right to vote. Sam's son Lyndon would sign both the Civil Rights Act and the Voting Rights Act as president of the United States—continuing his father's legacy of expanding access to the franchise.

8

The Border, Part 2

The fight for voting rights, however, is often push and pull—where steps forward in one place can lead to steps back in another. And that's what happened in the early twentieth century: while José Canales was making progress in the fight for justice in the state capitol, paranoia continued to rage along the border.

In 1917, U.S. authorities began delousing Mexican day laborers as they legally crossed at the port of entry at El Paso. The program would "bathe and disinfect all the dirty, lousy people who are coming into this country from Mexico," said a public health service official at the time. This same official admitted the risk of typhus was "not serious," but day laborers were nonetheless forced to strip naked and bathe in gasoline all the same.

Carmelita Torres, a seventeen-year-old who crossed from Juárez into El Paso, refused to submit to the humiliation. Instead, she led a protest that temporarily halted the delousing operation. The "bath riots," which took place at the El Paso–Juárez border, defied the soldiers sent to cow laborers into compliance. Not unlike the bus boycotts in the Deep South more than forty years later, Torres's refusal to submit to this dehumanizing indignity marked an important moment in the fight for justice and human rights on the border.

The racist insistence on portraying Mexican immigrants as a threat, whether as vectors for disease and crime or as a force that would undermine America, is not only wrong—it's the opposite of true.

Just two years after the bath riots, Marcelino Serna enlisted in the U.S. Army to join the American effort in World War I. When his drill sergeant learned that Serna was an undocumented immigrant from Chihuahua, he offered him a discharge from service. Serna refused and would go on to display uncommon valor and courage on the European battlefield, earning the Distinguished Service Cross, the second-highest military decoration awarded by the U.S. Army after the Medal of Honor.

Far from undermining America, Serna came back from that war as the most highly decorated soldier from the state of Texas.

This pattern of service and sacrifice would continue in World War II (with the all–Mexican American Company E, 141st Infantry), Vietnam (with the Bolaños brothers, the only four brothers to serve concurrently in that war), and more recent conflicts. Between 2013 and 2018, as this country fought the global war on terror, more than forty-four thousand noncitizens enlisted in the United States military. Nonetheless, more than a hundred of them have since been deported, unable to live in the country they were willing to die for.

This dissonance between the contributions of Mexican noncitizens and the way our government treats them is nothing new. While Marcelino Serna was serving during World War I, a new mayor was elected in El Paso on the promise of removing "undesirable Mexicans" from the community. This, along with a new state law that tightened voter eligibility, significantly depressed Mexican American electoral participation in El Paso.

If the goal was to diminish the political power of Mexican Americans, state-enforced voter suppression was clearly working. By 1922, roughly 80 percent of the El Pasoans paying poll taxes, and therefore eligible to vote, in the majority Mexican American city were Anglo.

But that wasn't enough for some people. During the same period, El Paso saw the rise of the Good Government League. A front for a growing Ku Klux Klan presence, the league stated that its purpose was to "keep aliens, illiterates and others who have no right to vote from entering the polls." The league mailed letters to suspected "aliens and illiterates" (who would presumably have someone read the letter to them) warning them not to vote. It also publicized a reward for those who could help with the convictions of illegal voters.

This all coincided with the rise of the Ku Klux Klan in the early 1920s all around the country, including in Texas. By 1922, the El Paso school board was dominated by members of the Klan who drummed out Catholic educators and renamed the community's schools for heroes of the Texas Revolution.

That same year, Texas sent Klansman Earle Mayfield to the U.S. Senate (with enough Klan-led voting irregularities to warrant a full, yearlong Senate investigation). Dallas, Fort Worth, and Wichita Falls all elected Klansmen as their mayors. The "imperial wizard" of the Klan was a dentist from Dallas. And when the Texas State Fair held

"Klan Day" in 1923, seventy-five thousand Klansmen and their families attended, ending the evening in front of a giant flaming cross.

Back in El Paso, the Frontier Klan No. 100 continued to infiltrate local centers of power: city hall, county government (the county treasurer boasted before a Baptist church congregation, "If you want to see a good Klansman, look at me"), the state legislative delegation, the El Paso police department, much of the leadership of the Protestant churches, and many prominent fraternal organizations.

They held massive initiation rites late into the night in El Paso's Franklin Mountains, with thousands of hooded men swearing allegiance to the Klan next to brightly burning clumps of kerosene-soaked cactus.

They violently terrorized Black Americans throughout the rest of the state—killing nine Black Texans in 1922 alone—but the Frontier Klan No. 100 in El Paso focused primarily on the persecution of Roman Catholics, the vigilante enforcement of vice laws (threatening El Pasoans who crossed into Juárez to evade Prohibition), and the pursuit of "voter fraud" by immigrants.

The Klan's Good Government League was involved in numerous altercations at polling locations during the 1922 election, with some involving violent coercion (described in the papers at the time as "gun play"). At certain polling sites, election judges mysteriously failed to appear, and members of the league, with the help of the county sheriff, elected their own replacements.

———

This ugly history is what makes Lawrence Nixon's stand against the white primary in El Paso all the more remarkable. Outside the Klan's power centers in Dallas and Fort Worth, El Paso hosted more Klan rallies than any other city in Texas.

The whites-only voting law, passed and signed in 1923, was motivated by the same paranoid hatred that targeted immigrants and Latinos throughout the borderlands and the same white supremacy that violently pushed African Americans from political participation—all coming from the same civic and political leaders who comprised the growing Klan membership throughout Texas. But Lawrence Nixon stood tall against it.

He knew that his fellow El Pasoans supported the Klan in significant numbers. He was aware of the reign of Klan terror across Texas and he was also aware that they were known to target Black doctors for humiliation and brutality. (A Houston Klansman castrated one Black dentist and tarred and feathered another.) And yet, even with this knowledge, knowing he could be killed for speaking out, Nixon exercised extraordinary courage in stepping forward to challenge the whites-only law.

Lawrence Nixon's bravery, patience, and tenacity would ultimately win the day when it came to ending the white primary. Texans of future generations would need to call on those qualities again and again to preserve those gains in the years to come.

———

In 1964, still bitter about the fact that President Kennedy and Vice President Johnson had won the state four years earlier, Texas Republicans launched a massive statewide voter intimidation operation, deploying more than ten thousand "poll watchers" in an attempt to intimidate likely Democratic voters from casting their ballots.

They created the "Harris County Negro Protective Association" to threaten Black voters with arrest if they tried to vote after having any interaction with law enforcement, including traffic violations. And in order to discredit any possible Democratic candidate's victory, the Harris County GOP would claim they had uncovered a conspiracy to commit voter fraud, as evidenced by a thousand "fictitious" voter registrations.

It goes to show that what's happening today in Texas is not without precedent.

As recently as 2018, the Texas secretary of state sent around a list of more than ninety thousand presumed illegal voters to county election officials. The secretary said he would mail the suspected voters a letter demanding they prove their citizenship—and if they failed to respond within thirty days, they would be purged from the rolls. However, it soon became apparent that many of the voters on the list were naturalized citizens, targeted only because of their previous immigration status.

The program was halted after the League of United Latin American Citizens (LULAC) successfully demonstrated that the state was trying to scare legal voters from participating in elections, prompting the secretary of state to resign. (It's worth noting that one of the founders of LULAC in 1929 was J. T. Canales, the former Texas state representative who had fought for accountability against the Texas Rangers and for voting rights for Mexican Americans while in the legislature.)

Nonetheless, a few years later, a new Texas secretary of state pursued yet another purge of suspected illegal voters, thanks to provisions in an elections bill passed that same year. County registrars throughout the state sent thousands of "challenge letters" to registered voters, requiring them once again to prove their citizenship within thirty days or forfeit their registration.

In November 2020, lieutenant governor Dan Patrick put one million dollars toward funding bounties for anyone able to produce proof of illegal voting—another historical echo of 1922. There was just one problem: actual voter fraud in Texas is nearly nonexistent. In the five-year period leading up to his offer, only fifty-five Texans had been prosecuted for voter fraud, out of seventeen million registered voters. That's a fraud rate of 0.00032353 percent. In fact, when Patrick finally paid out, it was to a man in Pennsylvania who nabbed a registered Republican who'd voted twice in the 2020 election.

But finding voter fraud wasn't the point of Lieutenant Governor Patrick's bounty. It was about spreading suspicion and fear—and creating the conditions that would allow for the introduction of increasingly proscriptive and suppressive voting laws.

There may be nothing new in the effort to scapegoat immigrants for political advantage and profit. But what *is* different about what's taking place in Texas now is this: the existential threat it poses to our democracy. If politicians can make us anxious and angry about immigrants—and scare us into believing that they are taking American jobs, committing crimes at a higher rate than native-born Americans, and changing the very character of our country—and then connect that to voting and elections, they can use that fabricated fear to rig the rules to stay in power.

———

This fear of democracy—of allowing the extraordinary, diverse population of Texas to be reflected in the political power of this state—is clearly not only a part of our history. It's part of who we are today.

The question is: Will it be part of our future?

On August 3, 2019—just over one hundred years after the massacre at Porvenir—a man drove six hundred miles across Texas to the Walmart in Central El Paso, with an AK-47-style semiautomatic rifle. He would later tell police that he came "to kill Mexicans."

The El Paso Fusion girls' soccer team was selling drinks and chicharrones at a table outside the Walmart to raise travel money for a tournament in Arizona. The shooter shot many of their parents and grandparents and then followed the young girls as they fled inside. In a matter of minutes, twenty people inside and outside of the store were dead and more than a dozen were seriously wounded. Two more people would die of their wounds in the coming days, and a third would die within the year.

The last to pass was Memo Garcia, the coach of the Fusion team and father to ten-year-old Karina and five-year-old Guillermo. He was kept alive for months after the shooting by caring doctors and nurses, the machines he was connected to, and the fierce love of his wife, Jessica. She had also been shot that day but had quickly recovered, immediately focusing on caring for her kids and posting vigil at Memo's side.

I got to spend time with her and Memo in that intensive care unit, watching him fight to live, watching her fight with him. Most people called Memo "Tank," both for his size and his indomitable spirit. But there was little his body could do against the high-impact, high-velocity round that had destroyed his internal organs. He died nine months after the attack.

The fear that attack would inspire would stay with the community long after. Alvaro Meno, whose seventy-eight-year-old father was also murdered, said he was "afraid to go out . . . because we feel like we are being hunted because of skin color."

I spent days and nights after the shooting with thousands of other El Pasoans and Juarenses at the makeshift memorial outside the Walmart. As Amy and I were walking back to our truck from the memorial one night, a young woman named Regina Hernandez approached and asked, "Do you remember me?"

I did. Her group, Mariachi Femenil, had performed at one of our events when I was in Congress.

We talked about the shooting, our deep sadness, and the beauty of so many people coming out to pay their respects on this night. The parking lot next to the Walmart was glowing with votive candles, humming with hushed prayers and every now and then music from those trying to lift our spirits.

Regina told me she didn't think she could continue performing as a mariachi, not after what happened at this Walmart.

"As mariachis, we are such an expression of Mexican identity and culture that we practically have a target on our backs."

In a manifesto the shooter posted just before entering the Walmart, he wrote that he was responding to the "Hispanic invasion of Texas." This, of course, was a key part of then-president Donald Trump's message of resentment and fear, which began the day he launched his campaign.

"When Mexico sends its people, they're not sending their best," he declared. "They're bringing drugs. They're bringing crime. They're rapists."

An investigation by *USA Today* after the El Paso shooting found that the president used words like "invasion," "alien," "killer," "predator," "criminal," and "animal" at his rallies to describe immigrants more than five hundred times.

At another rally, in Florida in May 2019, just three months before the El Paso shooting, the president rhetorically asked the assembled crowd how they were going to stop people from coming into the United States.

"Shoot them!" someone yelled in response.

The crowd cheered and the president laughed as he continued with his speech. His repeated warnings of invasion and the danger of Mexican and Latin American immigrants had found a receptive audience.

And not just in Florida. One day before the shooting in El Paso, Texas governor Greg Abbott mailed a fundraising appeal to his supporters, claiming they had an obligation to help repel illegal immigration.

"If we're going to DEFEND Texas," the letter begins, "we'll need to take matters into our own hands. . . ."

The El Paso shooter invoked the same logic as the president, the Texas governor, and the crowd at the Florida rally. "I am simply defending my country from cultural and ethnic replacement brought on by an invasion," he wrote.

He had been told repeatedly by those in power that we were being invaded, that we were essentially at war. That he was being "replaced." Repelling this invasion through force, with a weapon of war, only made sense to him.

He hoped that by murdering immigrants, or people who *looked* like immigrants, he could "remove the threat of the Hispanic voting bloc" before they "take control of the local and state government of my beloved Texas."

The shooter may never have heard of the massacre at Porvenir.

But the dynamics and motivations that produced the two largest massacres of Mexicans and Americans of Mexican descent are strikingly similar.

Fear of Mexicans and immigrants, stoked by politicians and the popular press and centering on a threatened "invasion," created the conditions for an extremely violent and twisted vigilante justice.

The El Paso shooter claimed in his manifesto that his planned massacre would be "an incentive that myself and many other patriotic Americans will provide" for "the Hispanic population . . . to return to their home countries."

That's literally what happened in Porvenir, Texas, in 1918. After the massacre there, the great majority of residents, by one count 140, left the small town for refuge in Mexico, removing the perceived threat and real power of those border residents.

The Walmart shooter wrote that he had given up on "peaceful means" of confronting this challenge, presumably through elections and our democracy. He feared that, as the Hispanic share of the population in Texas grew and as more immigrants received citizenship, Anglo Texans like him would no longer have political power and would be victims of a "political coup" of newly legalized Hispanic voters.

Unfortunately, despite the horrors of the El Paso terror attack, that way of thinking is still reflected by those in the highest positions of power in Texas.

A little more than two years after the El Paso shooting, Texas lieutenant governor Dan Patrick appeared on Fox News to renew the warnings of an invasion of immigrants and, in a chilling echo of the El Paso shooter, claimed that a "revolution" led by Democrats and undocumented immigrants was going to politically take over the country.

"When I say a revolution has begun, they are allowing this year, probably two million—that is who we apprehended, maybe another million—into this country. At least in eighteen years, even if they all don't become citizens before then and can vote, in eighteen years, every one of them has two or three children, you're talking about millions and millions and millions of new voters, and they will thank the Democrats and Biden for bringing them here."

Social scientists use the term "stochastic terrorism" to describe the public vilification of a group or community resulting in the incitement of a violent act. The stochastic terrorist does not say, "Kill this specific person in this place at this time"; instead he says, "We are being invaded and we must take matters into our own hands."

———

I recently reached out to Regina Hernandez. It had been two years since the young mariachi had approached me in the wake of the Walmart massacre.

It was clear that the attack had stayed with her and caused her to question her place in our country.

"It's kind of tough living in a world where people don't accept you," she told me. "I'm half Black and half Mexican. I feel very targeted. We have a bigger target because of our skin color, our heritage, our race. And I didn't know if a shooting like that would happen again. It was an eye-opener for me."

I told Regina that I remembered her saying that she and Mariachi Femenil might stop performing because of the attack—and asked if that ended up being the case.

"I still have that fear," she told me. "Two days ago, there was a gunman at a local high school, where one of my fellow mariachis is a teacher. It was shocking." She also still worries for her safety anytime she's in a crowded place. "I don't go to the Walmart where the shooting was. I won't even look at it."

And for a while, she did stop playing. "We said to ourselves, 'Let's give it a moment. Let's see what goes on. Let's focus on praying that the families of the victims are okay. Let's wait until we're not afraid.'"

But now?

"We've started playing again."

I asked her what made her decide to take this chance—despite what she and her fellow mariachis and the larger El Paso community have been through.

"In my family, mariachi, cumbias were part of my childhood," she explained. "They bring us a lot of joy, show us that we are an awesome race, heritage, and culture. Everything about who we are is beautiful. We're good people. You don't hear anything bad about El Paso or Mexican people here. The stereotypes come from the outside. Not every Mexican is a drug dealer, a rapist. The Mexican culture brings out who we really are.

"Whenever I play for someone, I am able to bring out this joy and pride, proud of who you are," she continued. "Proud of who *we* are. That's never going to change. El Paso is never going to change. We're never going to change. We're always going to be together.

"I kept playing because I like to see people happy," she said. "I want people to be proud of who they are."

There are those in this country who try to make us afraid of each other based on our differences. They do this to maintain and increase their power, to distract us from the real challenges and opportunities in front of us, to focus legitimate anger not at its cause but at those who are most defenseless against it. We see this in their hateful rhetoric, acts of terror, and attacks on rights—including the right to vote—directed at the marginalized and the vulnerable.

And then there are those who understand that the genius of America is that we are a people from all over the planet, who each contribute our unique cultures, experiences, and stories to the larger culture, experience, and story of America; that, at our best, we are able to peacefully and democratically resolve the natural conflicts and competitions that arise in a country this large and diverse; and even better, that we are at times able to come together to pursue a destiny not possible anywhere else precisely *because* we bring all of these differences to bear on the challenges before us.

Regina and the people I'm proud to call my neighbors in El Paso are a reflection of this genius. They ensure that we live our American values—e pluribus unum—in the example they set in their lives and through their contributions to the democracy that makes it all possible.

Should we succumb to those who would define us by our differences, who would stoke anger and direct it toward those they seek to disenfranchise; should we allow the demagogues and terrorists to win and thereby lose this form of government and the ability to freely and peacefully contribute our part to the greater whole, we will lose not only our democracy but that which makes America, America.

In the midst of the greatest division and conflict America had yet experienced, and one month before he would sign the Emancipation Proclamation, Abraham Lincoln presented a choice for the country, for his moment in time, and now for ours in his annual message to Congress in 1862: "We shall nobly save, or meanly lose, the last best hope of earth."

At every major turn of this country's course, we have been asked to make this choice between saving or losing our democracy. As Lyndon B. Johnson put it in his voting rights speech: "So it was at Lexington and Concord. So it was a century ago at Appomattox. So it was last week in Selma."

So it is now for us.

This form of government not only ensures our freedoms and our rights, it also sets America apart from almost the whole of human existence, and, as Lincoln and Johnson knew, it is a source of hope for so many around the world who live under tyranny.

And it is now on us once more to decide whether we shall resume the effort of enlarging and fortifying our democracy or lose this last best hope forever.

PART III

9

Overcoming

On July 22, 1944, Dr. Lawrence Nixon walked into Fire Station No. 5—the same polling place where he had been denied the right to vote twenty years earlier—and cast his ballot in the Democratic primary, a landmark victory in the fight for racial justice and the right to vote.

The Supreme Court battles initiated by Nixon and culminating in *Smith* would provide signal victories on the path toward other significant civil rights achievements like desegregating public schools in the following decade with *Brown v. Board of Education*. And the political success of Nixon's efforts would inform the greater fight for civil and voting rights in America, leading to the 1964 Civil Rights Act and the 1965 Voting Rights Act.

Nixon's story also reflected the essential spirit of El Paso—the spirit of *los de abajo,* the underdogs; the spirit that compels someone to look past their current circumstances, to somehow see over the mountain to pursue the potential beyond it, to define themselves not by what others would give them or name them but by what they could make possible themselves.

For me, El Paso can be summed up in Nixon saying "I've got to try" when others wanted to deny him the right to cast his ballot in 1924.

This city has always made its own luck. So physically and politically isolated from the rest of the country, El Paso has always had to look within itself and to its sister city of Juárez to find its strength and opportunity.

That Truman quote that I thought of at the train depot in Cooke County applies—we're not built on fear, but instead on an unbeatable determination to do the job at hand.

In 1949, five years after the *Smith* decision, Texas organized the first ever statewide boys' high school baseball championship. Bowie High was an unlikely challenger for the title. It was named a generation earlier by the Klan-controlled school board and located in South El Paso's impoverished Segundo Barrio. Nearly all of the student body was Mexican American and many were first-generation immigrants. Their parents worked the toughest, lowest-paying jobs in the community and their neighborhoods and schools lacked the resources that other parts of the city could take for granted.

Without money for uniforms, the team depended on the resourcefulness of the Bowie moms, who sewed jerseys and crafted gloves out of scrap material. It also helped that their coach, Nemo Herrera, believed in them.

Against the odds and under Herrera's leadership, Bowie bested the dominant El Paso schools like El Paso High and Ysleta and moved on to play for district and bi-district titles, winning those games as well.

They benefited from Herrera's constant training regimen, his deep personal investment in their success, and the fact that being from an immigrant-rich community was not a weakness, but a strength.

The semifinal game against Waco went into extra innings. With the score tied and the bases loaded, the Bowie team made the most of their bilingual border roots. Coach Herrera yelled to his catcher in Spanish that it looked like the Waco runner at third base was going to steal home. The Bowie catcher called for a pitch out, tagged the third-base runner, and then threw out the second-base runner, who was trying to steal third, setting up Bowie to win the game.

They headed to Austin to face the state's top-seeded high school. On the bus ride there, the Bowie team was met with signs that read NO DOGS OR MEXICANS ALLOWED. They ate their meals in restaurant kitchens, the owners and staff unwilling to seat them at tables with other guests.

In Lubbock, one of the team members was confounded by drinking fountain signs that read COLORED and WHITE.

"Being brown, I didn't know which was for me," he told *Sports Illustrated* writer Alexander Wolff.

On the night before the championship game, the Bowie team slept on cots underneath the stands at Memorial Stadium in Austin.

But the indignity they endured, the insults they bore along the way, never discouraged them or tempted them to despair.

They were focused on overcoming, on winning, on achieving their full potential and promise.

"It's not who you are or where you're from," their legendary coach, Nemo Herrera, would remind them. "It's who you become."

The next day, the Bowie Bears took the field against Austin, the hometown team that everyone expected would trounce these boys from El Paso.

And they played the game of their lives, defeating Austin and winning the state championship.

As Wolff recounts in his telling of the '49 Bears' triumph, these boys from Segundo Barrio had something else:

> The night before the team had left for Austin, students in a Bowie home economics class stayed up late preparing hard-boiled eggs for the players to eat on the trip. The Bears had won, one of those coeds would say at a Bowie reunion years later, "porque jugaron con huevos."

They knew they weren't supposed to win, weren't supposed to compete with the richer, whiter, bigger schools. But they had to try. They did, and they won.

———

It's that same spirit that helped Thelma White rise to the top of her class at the all-Black Douglass High School in El Paso—and led her to apply to Texas Western College in 1954.

Texas Western had never admitted a Black student—in part because the state college system held that *Brown v. Board of Education* did not apply to higher education. But Thelma White applied for admission anyway.

The school's registrar, Joseph Whitaker, denied her application after intense pressure from University of Texas System officials.

"One of the regents came to me and said, 'Whitaker, there's got to be a way you can keep these damn [expletive] out.'"

With the help of NAACP attorney Thurgood Marshall, chief of the NAACP Legal Defense and Educational Fund, White filed suit the next year, seeking to end the discriminatory admissions criteria at Texas Western. In doing so, she drew on the precedents of *Brown v. Board of Education* and victories won by the NAACP and Lawrence Nixon.

The federal judge hearing the case, El Pasoan R. E. Thomason, issued a ruling that summer that not only enjoined Texas Western from denying White admission but had the effect of ending segregation throughout public higher education in Texas. The benefits to Texas Western and El Paso came quickly.

———

In the fall of 1955, twelve Black students enrolled at Texas Western, the first successful integration of a Texas undergraduate college (among them was Mildred Parish Tutt, mother of U.S. congresswoman Barbara Lee).

The next year, Charles Brown joined the school's basketball team, the Miners, becoming the first African American to integrate college athletics in Texas.

Within a decade, the school hired Marjorie Lawson, who became the first Black faculty member in the University of Texas System.

The pace of progress and the accompanying pride in the achievements of previously marginalized communities extended beyond voting rights, athletics, and academia.

In 1957, Raymond Telles ran for mayor of El Paso, an audacious

undertaking, the same underdog spirit that animated Bowie's attempt to win the state baseball championship and Thelma White's
effort to enroll at Texas Western.

Since its founding in 1873, El Paso had never elected a Mexican American mayor. Nor had any other major American city. But
Telles, a World War II and Korean War veteran, had patiently and
persistently developed a political organization that would allow him
to overcome the de facto segregation of El Paso politics that had prevented meaningful Mexican American representation in positions of
public trust.

Along with his brother Richard, Telles invested his time and resources in registering Mexican American El Pasoans to vote and organized fundraisers to pay the poll taxes of lower-income voters.

His disciplined campaign, his spotless record of public service,
and his innovative effort to expand the electorate paid off, and on
Election Night, Telles won by a narrow margin.

R. E. Thomason, the same judge who ruled in Thelma White's
case, administered the oath of office to Telles in front of the largest
assembled crowd at city hall in El Paso history.

Telles served a successful first term, won reelection, and was then
asked by President John F. Kennedy to serve as ambassador to Costa
Rica, becoming the first Mexican American ambassador to any country from the United States.

But it was after Telles left for Central America that El Paso took
another big step forward in the fight for civil rights thanks to Bert
Williams, a young council member who had briefly served with
Telles.

Williams had grown up in Segundo Barrio, one of the few Anglo kids in this overwhelmingly Mexican American neighborhood.

Friends, mistaking his first name for "Bird," called him "Pájaro." Like Telles, he served in World War II, participating in the invasion of Okinawa. After the war, he played basketball at Texas Western College, and then after law school, he began playing competitive fast-pitch softball, winning two world championships. In fact, he later told reporters that part of the reason he ran for a seat on the El Paso City Council in the first place was to improve the quality of the city's ball fields.

It was on one of those softball fields that Williams developed a friendship with Nolan Richardson.

Like Williams, Richardson was one of the few kids without Mexican heritage who grew up in Segundo Barrio, but unlike Williams, Richardson was Black, significantly constraining the options open to him in the still-segregated South.

Even so, the racial discrimination in El Paso—most evident in his exclusion from public pools, restaurants, and movie theaters, as well as from academic and career opportunities—did not keep Nolan from extraordinary achievement. And neither did challenges in his family life. Despite the fact that his mother died when he was three, and that his father was an inconsistent presence in his life, Richardson was able to devote himself to school and athletics, rising to become a star basketball player at Bowie and then at Texas Western, playing for coach Don Haskins. Richardson would later become one of the best college basketball coaches in the country, winning the men's NCAA championship with Arkansas in 1994. He wasn't bad at softball, either.

So council member Williams recruited Richardson to play for one of his national championship softball teams. After a game one night in June 1962, Williams offered Richardson a ride home and, on the way, suggested stopping at the Oasis restaurant for a beer and a bite to eat. Richardson protested, warning Williams that as a Black man, he would not be served. But Williams insisted.

"We went inside," Williams told the *El Paso Times* years later, "and the waitress wouldn't even look at him. . . . She said, 'I can't serve him.' I told her, 'I'll see what I can do about that.'"

After the trip to the Oasis, Williams went to his city council office and began drafting a desegregation ordinance for the city of El Paso. When presented at the June 14 city council meeting, the ordinance passed unanimously only to be vetoed days later by Mayor Ralph Seitsinger, who insisted that integration must be voluntary and privately warned of the potential for rioting should the proposal become law.

This set up a showdown for the following council meeting, as Williams needed to keep a supermajority of his colleagues together to override the veto. Yet despite the controversy and the mayor's appeal to the safety and comfort of the status quo, Williams stayed the course.

Whether people were against it or for it, the integration vote was all anyone could talk about, and given the public interest in the measure, the council meeting was moved from city hall to the three-thousand-seat Liberty Hall. Even then, there weren't enough seats, and El Pasoans lined up on the sidewalks and streets nearby to hear the decision.

Williams and Seitsinger each made their case to their colleagues. The members of the city council took in the arguments, with deliberations lasting more than two hours before one of the council members made the motion to override the mayor's veto.

And then, each member cast their vote. One after another, they affirmed their support for integration and against the mayor's veto. El Paso and the cause of integration and justice won unanimously. The friendship between Bert Williams and Nolan Richardson, a white man and a Black man from the same Mexican immigrant neighborhood of Segundo Barrio, had produced a groundbreaking transformation in American civil rights.

El Paso would now officially become the first city in the former Confederacy to desegregate places of public accommodation, two years before the passage of the 1964 Civil Rights Act.

Supporters in the packed Liberty Hall erupted in applause and one of them, an unnamed Black woman, led the crowd in a rendition of "America the Beautiful." Lawrence Nixon's wife, Drusilla, was among those who sang along.

But she was not only a witness to this moment; like her husband, she had helped make it happen. She was an organizer on the Citizens' Committee on Human Relations that had formed to push the El Paso City Council to pass the desegregation ordinance.

———

El Paso's progress in civil rights made Don Haskins's job as the new coach of the Texas Western men's basketball team a lot easier.

Born in Enid, Oklahoma, Haskins had played college basketball at Oklahoma A&M, helping to lead the team to the NCAA semifinals in 1949 and 1951. His coaching career started in small Texas towns, like Benjamin, Hedley, and Dumas. In 1961, he agreed to take a pay cut in order to coach college ball in El Paso at Texas Western.

Thanks to Thelma White's effort to integrate the school, Texas Western had played a few Black players before Haskins's arrival, including Nolan Richardson. But it wasn't until the passage of the

El Paso integration ordinance that the school began to successfully recruit from across America. Haskins could now tell Black prospects that, unlike in other cities in the South, they would be able to sit in any seat at the movies, drink out of any water fountain at the park, and be served at any restaurant in town, including the Oasis Café.

Velvet James Barnes, an incredibly dexterous player better known as "Bad News," was Haskins's first big recruit. At six feet, eight inches, Barnes led the Texas Western Miners to their first NCAA tournament in 1963. The next year, he would be the first overall pick in the NBA draft, signing with the New York Knicks.

Other Black student athletes followed, and the quality of the Miners' program continued to improve. They finished the 1965–66 season with a 23–1 record and qualified for the NCAA tournament. There, they had the toughest games they'd played all year, including against Oklahoma City, the only team that had defeated them in the regular season. But they won them all, including an overtime game and a double-overtime game, to reach the championship final against the number one–ranked University of Kentucky.

Kentucky was a legendary basketball program thanks to coach Adolph Rupp, who had already won four national titles with the Wildcats and clearly expected to vanquish this no-name team from West Texas.

But Rupp had one big weakness as a coach: Though he had created a dominant national program, he'd failed to recruit a single Black player and wouldn't suit one up until 1971. He was missing the ability to see and attract talent regardless of race.

The Miners, meanwhile, had five Black players in their starting lineup.

With his Wildcats down three points at halftime, Rupp is alleged by former *Sports Illustrated* writer Frank Deford to have told his team: "You've got to beat those coons."

Though Kentucky would close within a point early in the second half, they would never take the lead and the Miners won the national championship game, 72 to 65.

Forty years later, Haskins would tell a reporter: "I really didn't think about starting five Black guys. I just wanted to put my five best guys on the court. I just wanted to win the game."

Texas Western's defeat of Kentucky marked the beginning of the end of racial segregation in college athletics. And it wouldn't have happened without the chain of events in El Paso over the prior forty years and the courageous leaders who'd preceded Haskins—the folks who fought for voting rights and secured a future where the government would be responsive to their needs.

When we fight—when, no matter what they tell us we can or can't do, we try anyhow—we make the impossible possible. That's Lawrence Nixon, Nemo Herrera, and the Bowie Bears. That's Thelma White, Raymond Telles, Bert Williams, and Nolan Richardson. That's the '66 Miners. That's El Paso. And that's America.

But there's another side to our story, too—the price we pay when we don't fight, when we accept the fate that's been written for us by others.

———

The day before the 1966 NCAA tournament started, Lawrence Nixon died from injuries he sustained in a car crash. Surrounded by his family, this elder statesman of Texas civil and voting rights passed away in his adopted hometown of El Paso.

It was the death of a giant and it coincided with the end of an era.

Though there would be moments of extraordinary leadership with national implications in El Paso following Nixon's death—the Chicano movement and the breakthrough strike at the Farah factory in the 1970s are big examples—El Paso soon began to lose its pride of place as a national leader in civil and voting rights.

Comfortable in the success that had accrued from its previous years as the epicenter of trade and industry in the Southwest, satisfied by the moral victories from prior decades, and economically stagnant as a result, El Paso slowed its stride, adapted to the status quo, and chose comity and comfort over confrontation.

You could actually measure the decline. Our per capita income against the national average fell; our levels of educational attainment paled in comparison to the rest of the country; our voter turnout numbers dropped to among the lowest in the state.

But you could also feel it.

I grew up in the 1970s and '80s in El Paso. In classrooms at Mesita Elementary and El Paso High School, I never heard of, nor was I taught about, the '49 Bears or Carmelita Torres and the bath riots of 1917. Marcelino Serna, the immigrant who came back a hero from World War I, was unknown to me. And so was Lawrence Nixon.

What I did know was that El Paso wasn't fulfilling its purpose or its potential. You could tell that there was greatness in our past—from the epic art deco buildings downtown to the reverence with which people treated Don Haskins, who was still coaching when I went to Miner games as a kid, to the pride with which El Pasoans of a much older generation carried themselves. But that greatness was not evident in the El Paso that raised my generation. I felt something as a young man in El Paso that I couldn't articulate then, but I can see clearly now: we had lost our way.

We became a city that accepted a fate decided by others, a city that didn't know its own history—one that became subject to the stories that other people in other cities would tell about us.

This beautiful binational community, whose border neighborhoods had served as the Ellis Island for the immigrants of the Americas—whose residents had led democratic revolutions in Mexico, whose leaders had changed the course of civil rights in the United States—wasn't standing up for itself, wasn't telling its own story, wasn't learning its own history.

We had squandered the inheritance left by those who came before us. Not only did that dishonor their sacrifices and service, but it left us vulnerable to those who would take advantage of and use this community for dark purposes. Our history, our true story was the protection against the dangers generated by ignorance and lies. When we stopped telling our own story—because we'd lost the thread and couldn't pass it on to the next generation—other people told it for us. In the new telling, El Paso became a "dangerous" outpost, a source of threats instead of opportunities.

At the State of the Union address in February 2019, Donald Trump described El Paso as a violent city with one of the highest rates of crime in the country.

He looked into the camera and told the sixteen million Americans watching that El Paso was one of "the nation's most dangerous cities." He said only extreme measures, like building a wall, would make it safe.

But here's the truth: El Paso was ranked among the safest cities in America in 2019, and for many years before that—long before any wall with Mexico was built. In fact, violent crime increased during the wall's construction and after it was completed.

Six months after Trump's incendiary speech—and after years of his baseless lies about violent immigrants in places like El Paso—a gunman killed twenty-three innocent people because he believed the fictions being spun by those in power.

In a peaceful city that usually saw no more than twenty people killed in a year, twenty-three El Pasoans were murdered in a matter of minutes. The lie that we were dangerous, deadly, and violent, unchallenged by the truth that we were none of those things, ended up producing the very death and violence Trump had made up.

That's why we have to know our history. That's why we have to tell our stories—to ourselves and to those we've never met. And it's why we must connect what's happening today with what has happened before. Because that's the only way to learn from our past, to use those lessons to get through the challenges we face in the present, and to build on that progress so that we live up to our true potential in the years to come.

10

Forward

Lawrence Nixon had the courage to fight a vicious and violent system of caste and segregation in Texas elections—and he had the tenacity to stay in that fight for the twenty long years it took to win it.

What made that possible was his faith—his faith in himself and in the possibility of America becoming a true democracy, even if he didn't know when or how it would happen. I'm sure there were days when he wondered if he would live to see the progress for which he was fighting, but regardless of what stood in his way, he never wavered from the sentiment he expressed election after election at the fire station upon being told they could not let him vote: "I've got to try."

Do we share that faith in democracy? That belief that, despite the obstacles in our way, we have to try?

The presidential election of 2020 was arguably the most consequential since 1864, where the stakes for the Union were nothing less than winning the Civil War or surrendering. Democracy was on the ballot in 2020, and still, in Texas, more than seven million who were eligible to vote never cast a ballot.

Why? There's a temptation to blame nonvoters. How could you—in the world's greatest democracy, a democracy that courageous Americans literally gave their lives to establish, expand, and defend—not vote?

Is it laziness or lack of civic responsibility? Is it complacency or apathy?

Or could it be something else?

History and the facts of our current situation show us that it is definitely something else.

Voting rights champions like Lawrence Nixon, J.T. Canales, Lonnie Smith, Lyndon Johnson, and Barbara Jordan helped make illegal much of the violence and suppression that kept African Americans, Mexican Americans, and other minority groups from the ballot box. But their victories were neither complete nor final, and in the intervening years, Texas began to lurch back toward suppression.

Since the *Shelby* ruling in 2013, our state legislature has ushered in a new wave of voting laws designed to keep certain Texans from voting.

It began with the most restrictive voter identification law in the country, enacted months after the *Shelby* ruling. That bill declared that you could prove your identity at a polling place with a Texas handgun carry license but not with a state-issued student ID card. The partisanship of the measure wasn't subtle. It was overt, blocking six hundred thousand registered voters from accessing the ballot box.

The effects of this suppression were compounded by gerryman-dered maps designed to dilute the power of Black and Latino voters across the state. In fact, the redistricting was so blatant in its effort to disenfranchise voters of color that in 2017, a three-judge federal panel, two members of which were nominated by Republican presi-dents, called the state's maps a "racial gerrymander."

Gary Bledsoe, the president of the Texas NAACP, described the new maps as vastly diminishing "the voting strength of minorities all around the state."

The goal was to "pack" or "crack" minority voters. In some places, partisans redrew the electoral map to "pack" more voters of color into the same district, making the surrounding districts safe conservative territory. In other places, they did the inverse. They "cracked" up the voters of color, distributing them so thinly among various districts that these voters effectively had no power. (Why did seven million eligible Texans decide not to vote in the 2020 election? Well, many saw it for what it was: an election where some voters counted more than others.)

It only got worse after the 2020 Census. During the 2010s, Texas grew by more than four million people, with minority residents rep-resenting 95 percent of that growth. But when the Texas legislature unveiled their new district voting maps, the number of Hispanic-majority districts dropped from eight to seven and there was not a single Black-majority congressional district.

———

This was the first redistricting in fifty-five years without preclearance. After Lyndon Johnson signed the Voting Rights Act in 1965, each time Texas wanted to redraw its districts, or move a polling place, or change registration requirements, the state had to clear its plans with the Department of Justice to ensure they passed legal muster. And each time, Justice would correct Texas's plans to ensure that minority voting power was not diluted, that certain Texans weren't drawn out of districts to minimize the impact of their votes, and that, intentionally or not, Texans weren't denied their constitutional rights to equal treatment under the law.

When the Supreme Court handed down the *Shelby* decision, it threw out the preclearance provision. Now, Texas legislators can basically do whatever they want, not only through redistricting but also through old-school voter suppression.

In the years since *Shelby* was decided, more than seven hundred polling places in Texas have closed, double the number of the next closest state—despite the fact that Texas has added more people than any other state. Most of these closures have been concentrated in the fastest-growing Black and Latino neighborhoods.

So, when we see voters lined up six hours deep on Election Day outside Texas Southern University, a historically Black institution, we should see this not simply as a demonstration of persistence but also as a deeply shameful indication of how broken Texas's voting system is.

For every person who could wait for six hours in line to vote, how many physically could not manage the same feat?

How many could not get six hours' leave from work to wait?

How many simply refuse to put up with the indignity of waiting for half a day in order to cast their ballot?

The answer to why more Texans don't vote is not complacency, nor is it apathy.

And it is not by accident that Texas has one of the lowest levels of voter turnout in the country.

It is by design.

In fact, according to the voting rights scholar Ari Berman, Texas is the toughest state in which to vote. Voter ID, racial gerrymandering, and the mass closure of polling places have a lot to do with it, but there are a number of smaller nefarious obstacles that give the Lone Star State such an ignominious distinction.

For example, unlike almost every other state in the country, Texas does not allow you to register to vote online. There is essentially nothing you can't do online in Texas, or anywhere in America today, except register to vote. And in the middle of a pandemic that has killed more than eighty-seven thousand Texans, the governor chose to limit ballot drop-off boxes to one per county, including in giant urban counties like Harris, which has 4.7 million people.

———

But there's one provision of the elections code, added in 2021, that is just a half step from some of Texas's grimmest history. It allows partisan poll watchers, "concerned citizens," to monitor and intimidate voters, with nearly unchecked power, at polling places throughout the state.

The goal is to make it harder to vote, to intimidate certain voters from voting so that those in power can stay in power. This is the kind of thing that Texas officeholders will even brag about. On January 6, 2021, hours before Donald Trump incited an insurrection during a speech on the National Mall, Texas's attorney general—a man named Ken Paxton—was on the same "Stop the Steal" rally stage, boasting about how he'd made it harder for Texans to vote in the 2020 election.

He told the crowd, "Because of those efforts, Donald Trump won Texas by over six hundred thousand votes." He's the same attorney general who sued to overturn election results in four states that Trump lost.

And Paxton wasn't the only Texas official involved in the effort to overturn the election. Houston-area state representative Briscoe Cain flew to Philadelphia to join Trump's legal team as they sought to find evidence that would overturn the results in Pennsylvania.

Thankfully, they did not succeed. But while the efforts to overturn the 2020 election ended on January 6, along with the lives of two Capitol police officers, killed at the hands of whipped-up insurrectionists, Paxton and Cain found a way to perpetuate the spirit of the attempted coup in other forms.

In February, the speaker of the Texas House named Cain chair of the House Elections Committee and tasked him with rewriting the state's election laws.

The bill he wrote, a later draft of which ended up becoming law, added even more obstacles to voting in Texas—like mandating that Texans with disabilities produce additional verification of their identity to vote by mail and limiting their ability to ask for help when voting in person.

In fact, the new state law made it harder for everyone to vote by mail, because it makes election workers and county clerks who want to facilitate mail-in voting subject to criminal charges!

It also contains the aforementioned poll-watching provisions, which echo some of the darkest chapters of Texas history.

Proponents of the law, like Cain and Paxton, defended these policies by saying they were passed to combat voter fraud, but there's proof that's not the case: While the legislature was still debating the bill, Harris County GOP officials let the mask slip. A leaked Zoom video shows them trying to recruit ten thousand poll watchers for an "election integrity brigade."

Would the brigade focus on integrity everywhere in Harris County, which includes the city of Houston? No.

The GOP officials wanted only to focus on Houston's diverse urban core, places like Wheeler Avenue Baptist Church, a Black congregation famous for hosting Martin Luther King Jr. and a leading civil rights institution. The "integrity brigade" is reminiscent of the "Harris County Negro Protective Association" of 1964 or the Klan's Good Government League of the 1920s or the Loyalty Rangers of the 1910s. It might be why some people refer to efforts like these as "Jim Crow 2.0."

After all, if you really were using poll watchers to combat voter fraud, why would you only send them to precincts whose residents are Black? The answer is that you wouldn't. And the goal of this bill wasn't to ensure election integrity. The goal was to finish what had been started on January 6.

And though bills like this were not limited to Texas—dozens of other states changed their election laws in the aftermath of 2020, cheered on by the former president—only Texas was willing to go to this extreme. In fact, the bill was so egregious that Democratic members of the legislature, including some who were willing to negotiate the particulars to find some consensus, walked out en masse during the final hours of the regular session, denying Cain and the Republicans a quorum and temporarily killing the legislation.

But despite Democrats' best efforts, including leaving Texas altogether at the start of a special legislative session called to pass the bill, they were unable to prevail, and by the fall of 2021, a state that was already the toughest in which to vote became known as the most successful in suppressing voters.

———

While not as violent or overt as historical attempts at voter suppression, like the Loyalty Rangers of the Rio Grande Valley or the Klansmen who patrolled polling places throughout the state, the intent is the same: depress political participation among some groups of Texans to elevate the political power of others.

And like the Texas Election Outrage of 1886, when Black poll workers were killed and ballot boxes were stolen in Washington County, what's happening in Texas now commands the nation's attention. Congress has convened hearings on the new Texas law, newspapers have made this a front-page story, and President Biden has engaged in the fight, calling Texas voter suppression attempts "an assault on democracy that we've seen far too often this year—and often disproportionately targeting Black and Brown Americans."

And just as in the nineteenth century, there is once again federal legislation that could help combat this suppression.

In 2019, Maryland congressman John Sarbanes introduced the For the People Act, which includes provisions for automatic voter registration, making Election Day a national holiday, and replacing gerrymandered districts with those drawn by nonpartisan redistricting commissions.

Texas wasn't the original impetus for the For the People Act. But by 2021, after its voter suppression bill was signed into law, Texas became its case in point.

And yet, as happened with the Federal Elections Bill of 1890, there has once again been a lack of political will to pass the necessary protections to save our democracy. Even though the pro-democracy party (this time, it's the Democrats) has a majority in both chambers of Congress, and even though that same party controls the White House with a president who campaigned to improve voting rights, it has been unable to pass the For the People Act or other voting rights bills, like the John Lewis Voting Rights Advancement Act and the Freedom to Vote Act.

Five months before the election, President Biden made a promise to voters: "One thing the Senate and the president can do right away is pass the bill to restore the Voting Rights Act. . . . It's one of the first things I'll do as president if elected. We can't let the fundamental right to vote be denied." And yet, nearly a year and a half into his presidency, there has been little progress made and the issue has not become central to his agenda, overtaken by the pressing needs of the pandemic and the country's economic recovery.

Not that it would be easy to pass voting rights. The president must overcome skepticism and outright intransigence among some members of his own party in the Senate, and even if he were to satisfy outstanding concerns there, he would still have to convince them to bypass the filibuster. It's a tall order, but as Adam Jentleson, who has chronicled the history of the Senate filibuster, put it, while the president may give it his all and fail, "the stakes are so high, he has to try."

After the 1890 Federal Elections Bill died on the horns of a Texas-led filibuster, it would be seventy-five years before another major voting rights bill finally succeeded. And in the interim, our democracy collapsed.

Will that be our fate once again? Will we refuse to act and

continue this descent into something that no longer resembles a democracy? Or will we seize the opportunity before us now to once again secure voting rights?

Are we 1890 or 1965?

The question is ours to answer. But I am confident that Texas—as it did in the aftermath of the "Outrage" of 1886, as it did in the courage shown by Lawrence Nixon in 1924, and as it did by shaping and inspiring Lyndon Johnson's leadership on the Voting Rights Act in 1965—will play a critical role in deciding what comes next.

Epilogue

While in Fort Worth earlier this year, I met another native of Marshall, Texas.

Born two years after Lawrence Nixon began his fight for the right to vote, Opal Lee (née Flake) grew up in East Texas and moved to Fort Worth when she was ten years old. In 1939, a few years after her family arrived in North Texas, her parents purchased a home in a predominately white neighborhood on East Annie Street. This was relatively unprecedented for an African American family like hers at the time.

On June 19 of that year, a mob of hundreds of white rioters raided the family's home, terrorizing twelve-year-old Opal and her siblings, burning their furniture, and threatening their lives. In the midst of the attack, Lee's father grabbed his shotgun but was warned by the Fort Worth police officers on the scene that if he were to use it, they would turn the mob loose on his family. The attackers ultimately burned the house to the ground.

It was no accident that the mob had chosen this day, of all days, to attack Opal's family. It was June 19, widely celebrated by Black Americans as Juneteenth, a commemoration of emancipation coming to Texas.

Exactly seventy-four years earlier, almost two and a half years after the Emancipation Proclamation was issued by President Abraham Lincoln and more than two months after General Robert E. Lee surrendered at Appomattox, Union general Gordon Granger read General Order No. 3 on June 19, 1865, in Galveston: "The people of Texas are informed," he declared, "that in accordance with a proclamation from the Executive of the United States, all slaves are free."

On the anniversary of that day in 1939, as Black Texans celebrated their liberation, a mob of white Texans in Fort Worth tried to ensure that they didn't feel too free.

The Associated Press reported that "violence climaxed observance of Negro emancipation late tonight when a crowd estimated at 500 persons stormed the residence of Otis Flake."

That moment forever changed Opal Lee and her understanding of Juneteenth.

"The fact that it happened on the nineteenth day of June has spurred me to make people understand that Juneteenth is not just a festival," she said from the steps of her historic Fort Worth home during a speech in early June 2020.

In fact, from 1939 forward, in her roles as an educator, a civic leader, and a volunteer at her local food pantry, she has helped Texans understand the deeper lessons of Juneteenth and our country's history. Juneteenth, she taught, shouldn't be a celebration only for African Americans or Texans. It should be a day that helps Americans from every background understand that this country's history belongs to *all* of us and that our future as a country depends on *each* of us. We're connected, she'd say, there's no getting past that.

"The slaves didn't free themselves," she explains. "It took all kinds of people—Quakers, abolitionists—to get the slaves free.

"We all want the same thing. So why can't we unite and address these disparities that we know exist?"

At the age of eighty-nine, Opal Lee decided to take the conversation beyond her hometown—traveling the fourteen hundred miles from Fort Worth to Washington, D.C., to bring attention to Juneteenth. Every morning and every afternoon, she walked two and a half miles—five miles a day—all with the goal of making Juneteenth a federal holiday.

I asked her if she thought she'd be successful at the time.

"No, not in my lifetime," she told me. "But I had to try."

She told her story along the way, talking with and listening to people all over the country. She pled her case before members of Congress and Presidents Obama and Biden. And eventually, her persistence, her courage, and her story finally paid off.

On June 17, 2021, President Joe Biden signed the Juneteenth National Independence Day Act into law, making Juneteenth the first new federal holiday in thirty-eight years. Opal Lee sat in the front row at the bill signing ceremony and received a standing ovation from the assembled dignitaries.

In his remarks, the president credited her with paving the way for the new holiday, and he talked about the work necessary to achieve true equality in America.

"The promise of equality is not going to be fulfilled . . . so long as the sacred right to vote remains under attack. We see this assault from restrictive laws, threats of intimidation, voter purges, and more—an assault that offends our very democracy. We can't rest until the promise of equality is fulfilled for every one of us in every corner of this nation.

"That, to me," the president concluded, "is the meaning of Juneteenth."

Opal Lee agreed. In a speech the year before, recounting the burning of her home and her work to help America meet the promise of emancipation, she called on her fellow Texans to make themselves heard through our democracy.

"When you go out and vote—when you make the changes—we can keep America from burning."

At a time when we may wonder whether our democracy can make it—after the insurrection attempt on January 6, 2021, the hundreds of voter suppression bills introduced across dozens of state legislatures since then, and the rise in political terrorism like the 2019 murders in El Paso—we can be tempted to despair.

But then I think about what Opal Lee faced in 1939, when the mob burned her home down, wondering whether things could ever be made right. And I think about how Lawrence Nixon was denied the right to vote year after year after year during the "white primary" era. Nixon and Lee didn't just wonder, or fret, or complain. They found that the antidote to despair is action. And action, even in the face of seemingly impossible odds, can bring victory.

The challenge we must accept is not only to go out and vote, but to make sure every eligible American can do the same. If our history has taught us anything, it is that democracy is never guaranteed. The fight is never fully won. And while progress is always possible, backsliding, suppression, and even violence are inevitable unless we consciously commit ourselves to the work before us. We are always becoming a democracy; it never ends. It can be exhausting, daunting, even brutal work. But compared to the alternative? We don't have a choice.

Lawrence Nixon understood this. It's also what the Mexican American kids from Bowie High School in El Paso fought and died for when they became the men of Company E in World War II. It was realized in the election of Raymond Telles; in the desegregation of Texas higher education thanks to Thelma White and Thurgood Marshall; and in Lyndon Johnson's successful push for national voting rights. Opal Lee has lived it from that June night in 1939 right through to today.

We must embrace the challenges before us. Because our democracy, which makes everything that is essential to this country possible, is on the line. And while the outcome of the fight before us might be uncertain, we know one thing for sure. We've got to try.

Acknowledgments

Thank you, Zachary Wagman, for editing and guidance; Maggie Walsh, for research, diligence and direction; Will Guzmán, for writing the essential book on Lawrence Nixon and helping me understand his larger role in American civil and voting rights; Tayhlor Coleman, for sharing her story and connecting it to our history (and getting out there to register voters!); Powered by People volunteers and those of other great Texas voting rights organizations, for doing the work; Robert Gunn, for encouragement, feedback, and insight; Sam Koppelman, for suggestions on the final draft; Raymond Telles, for resources and feedback; Brett Pelham, for research and data help; Amy, for reading and giving much-needed constructive criticism; and other readers who helped make this better: Mike Stevens, Cynthia Cano, Susie Byrd, Pat Ledbetter, Steve Ortega, Ulysses O'Rourke, Veronica Escobar. Thank you, Craig, Mollie, and David, for helping to make this happen. Thank you, Edna McIver, for spending time

ACKNOWLEDGMENTS

with me and helping me better understand your extraordinary parents; Gus Sambrano, rest in peace, the '49 Bears shortstop, for telling me the story of the team, and Alex Wolff, for bringing it to a national audience; Opal Lee, for sharing her story and being so incredibly encouraging; Jessica, Guillermo, and Karina, the strongest people I know; Ari Berman and Adam Jentleson, for trying to wake up America; Jenika, Judge Shuster, Auden, Courtney, Sherman, Pablo Gonzales, Judge George, for being great examples of public service and proving that democracy is worth fighting for; Regina, for not giving in; Luis and Marcela and other survivors who demonstrate the strength and power of this community; and the people of El Paso and Texas, for helping this country come through.

Notes

PROLOGUE

1   **So it was an odd time:** The details of the attack were recorded during testimony and Senate debate over voting rights atrocities in the Southern United States and found in the *Congressional Record*. See *Congressional Record: Containing the Proceedings and Debates of the Fifteenth Congress, First Session,* vol. 19, part 9, for Sep. 27, 1888 (Washington, D.C.: Government Printing Office, 1888). Available at books.google .com.

2   **In the struggle:** Robert W. Shook, "The Texas 'Election Outrage' of 1886," *East Texas Historical Journal* 10, no. 1, article 7 (1972), https:// scholarworks.sfasu.edu/ethj/vol10/iss1/7 (accessed Feb. 9, 2022).

3   **"Things here look gloomy":** *Congressional Record,* Sep. 27, 1888, 9006.

3   **"While all good citizens":** Shook, "The Texas 'Election Outrage' of 1886."

3   **"The hanging":** Ibid.

NOTES

7   **guaranteeing the franchise:** The Reconstruction legislative efforts to guarantee the franchise were tortured at best. President Andrew Johnson himself threw up roadblock after roadblock. He pardoned ex-Confederates who openly supported Black Codes used by Southern states to restrict the labor and civil rights of Blacks. He also vetoed equal rights, economic, and education assistance bills (the Freedmen's Bureau Bill and Civil Rights Act). Even though the pro–civil rights Republicans who dominated Congress repassed both, and adopted the Fourteenth Amendment (which extended citizenship to African Americans and recognized their right to due process and equal protection under the law), they did not extend voting rights. All the Fourteenth Amendment did was penalize states that deprived males over twenty-one of their votes by proportionately reducing their representation in Congress. However, it was never enforced. It is also important to recognize that the Reconstruction statutes applied only to Southern Blacks; most in the North still could not vote. For example, from 1865 to 1868, Connecticut, Kansas, Michigan, New York, Ohio, and Wisconsin voted against referenda to enfranchise Blacks. In 1870, the Fifteenth Amendment, also a compromise, guaranteed protection against racial discrimination in voting but did not affirmatively grant universal suffrage to Black male adults, and its protections did not include the "nonracial" qualifications like literacy tests and poll taxes. For a full discussion, see Susan Cianci Salvatore, ed., *Civil Rights in America: Racial Voting Rights*, National Historic Landmarks Program, Cultural Resources, National Park Service (Washington, D.C.: U.S. Department of the Interior, 2007, rev. ed. 2009), https://www.nps.gov/subjects/tellingallamericansstories/upload/CivilRights_VotingRights.pdf, 5–6.

8   **In 1871, the leading:** Ibid., 5, 10.

9   **Panic of 1873:** Called the "Long Depression" now to differentiate it from the Great Depression, the Panic of 1873 had three major causes: the U.S. financed the tremendous cost of the Civil War by issuing millions in "greenbacks" (paper money), that were, for the first time, not backed by physical gold and silver; speculation by European and American banks in the growing U.S. railroad industry; and an international

money shortage when Germany adopted a gold-only standard (rather than gold and silver) for its currency. Beginning with a bank failure in Austria, the depression came to the U.S. when banks began calling in their loans to the railroads. The railroads failed, as did the banks. This led to a prolonged (more than ten years) economic slowdown after the panic itself (runs on the banks, etc.). See History Central, "Economic Panic of 1873," https://www.historycentral.com/rec/EconomicPanic .html#:~:text=Railroad%20construction%20halted%20nationwide%20 as,that%20lasted%20almost%2010%20years.

9   **"Let the people"**: Shook, "The Texas 'Election Outrage' of 1886," 25.

11   **a "new power"**: Paula J. Giddings, "A Noble Endeavor: Ida B. Wells-Barnett and Suffrage," National Park Service, https://www.nps.gov /articles/000/a-noble-endeavor-ida-b-wells-barnett-and-suffrage.htm.

11   **Between 1961 and 1969:** Tomiko Brown-Nagin, "The Transformation of a Social Movement into Law? The SCLC and NAACP's Campaigns for Civil Rights Reconsidered in Light of the Educational Activism of Septima Clark," *Women's History Review* 8, no. 1 (1999), https://www .tandfonline.com/doi/pdf/10.1080/09612029900200193 (accessed Feb. 10, 2022), 95.

11   **Bob Moses:** German Lopez, "How the Voting Rights Act Transformed Black Voting Rights in the South, in One Chart," *Vox,* Aug. 6, 2015, https://www.vox.com/2015/3/6/8163229/voting-rights-act-1965 (accessed Feb. 10, 2022).

12   **"We've got to get":** Jesse J. Holland, "Things to Know About the Voting Rights Act of 1965," Associated Press, Aug. 5, 2015, https://apnews.com /article/ac55149b65544f4c8d2439ca6c2d831f (accessed Feb. 10, 2022).

13   **"At times, history and fate":** "Transcript of the Johnson Address on Voting Rights to Joint Session of Congress," *New York Times,* Mar. 16, 1965, https://www.nytimes.com/1965/03/16/archives/transcript-of -the-johnson-address-on-voting-rights-to-joint-session.html.

15   **"Your speech to the joint session of Congress":** Sam Levine, "Fight to Vote: Activism Works—Just Look at the 1965 Voting Rights Act," *The*

NOTES

Guardian, Feb. 18, 2021, https://www.theguardian.com/us-news/2021
/feb/18/fight-to-vote-newsletter-voting-rights-act-history (accessed
Feb. 10, 2022).

1: "I'VE GOT TO TRY"

23   **The year before, free from any federal voting rights:** SB 44 CH 32,
Texas General Laws, 38th 2nd Called Session, https://lrl.texas.gov
/scanned/sessionLaws/38-2/SB_44_CH_32.pdf.

24   **wrote one dentist:** Will Guzmán, *Civil Rights in the Texas Borderlands:
Dr. Lawrence Nixon and Black Activism* (University of Illinois Press,
2015), 47.

27   **recruited Chick Brandom:** Cameron L. Saffell, "El Paso Celebrates New
Mexico and Arizona Statehood," *Southern New Mexico Historical Review*
(2012), https://www.donaanacountyhistsoc.org/HistoricalReview/2012
/HistoricalReview2012.htm.

27   **He soon despaired:** Guzmán, *Civil Rights in the Texas Borderlands*, 25.

27   **More than five hundred:** "Negro Brute Lynched," *Austin American
Statesman*, Nov. 5, 1907, detailing the lynching of Alex Johnson. Found
at http://www.lynchingintexas.org/files/show/1960.

28   **another lynching of a Black man:** "Mob Storms Jail in Texas: Negro
Lynched," *Albuquerque Journal*, Dec. 21, 1909, detailing the lynching
of Louis "Coke" Mills. Found at http://www.lynchingintexas.org/files
/show/43.

28   **"It was strange to find":** Guzmán, *Civil Rights in the Texas Borderlands*, 46.

29   **Nixon was elected:** Will Guzmán, "Border Physician: The Life of Lawrence A. Nixon, 1883–1966," Ph.D. dissertation, University of Texas
at El Paso, Dec. 2010, 76, https://digitalcommons.utep.edu/open_etd
/2495.

NOTES

29   **Nixon and his son:** Guzmán, *Civil Rights in the Texas Borderlands*, 48.

30   **taking Nixon's wife:** Conrey Bryson, *Dr. Lawrence A. Nixon and the White Primary*, Southwestern Studies no. 42 (University of Texas at El Paso, 1974), 26.

30   **Will Guzmán, who wrote:** Guzmán, *Civil Rights in the Texas Borderlands.*

31   **And he voted:** Bryson, *Dr. Lawrence A. Nixon and the White Primary*, 6.

32   **enshrining the prohibition:** Guzmán, *Civil Rights in the Texas Borderlands*, 79.

32   **they had to be a consistently registered Democrat:** While there were Republicans in Texas at this time, the Democratic Party primary was decisive if you wanted to choose your county commissioner, congressman, governor, and so on. Republicans were few enough that they lacked the critical mass to trigger Republican primary elections in some years. L. W. Washington, a Nixon contemporary, said about El Paso Black residents' sentiments about Nixon's willingness to be the test case: "During our fourteen years residence in El Paso, we have not been denied the right to vote in any election until July 26, 1924 . . . since no other party has been strong enough here to make a showing at the polls, the elections for city, county and state officers, for the most part, have been held with one faction of the Democrats against another . . . the Negro vote had been sought and his vote the last fourteen years has been cast for those whom he knew to be better disposed for the entire citizenship." Darlene Clark Hine, Steven F. Lawson, and Merline Pitre, *Black Victory: The Rise and Fall of the White Primary in Texas* (University of Missouri Press, 2003), 114. The white primary laws, then, effectively disenfranchised Black Texans completely.

32   **"who is not afraid":** Bryson, *Dr. Lawrence A. Nixon and the White Primary*, 17.

32   **"I know you can't":** Ibid., 23.

NOTES

2: THIS TIME, THEY VOTED

34 **Nixon and Knollenberg appealed:** It had been their strategy all along to get to the Supreme Court by the shortest possible route. The case was dismissed without explanation as to the merits and Knollenberg and an associate filed an assignment of errors and petition for a writ of error before the same court. The district judge who had dismissed the case granted an order that the case be heard before the Supreme Court on a writ of error. This allowed a direct appeal to the Supreme Court, without a stopover at the U.S. Court of Appeals. See Bryson, *Dr. Lawrence A. Nixon and the White Primary*, 34–35.

35 **"We find it unnecessary":** Nixon v. Herndon, 273 U.S. 536 (1927).

35 **"the most significant case":** *El Paso Herald*, Mar. 7, 1927. Cited in Bryson, *Dr. Lawrence A. Nixon and the White Primary*, 45.

35 **"I had rather take":** Supreme Court of the United States, October Term, 1931, No. 265, L. A. Nixon, Petitioner, against James Condon and C. H. Kolle, Respondents, Brief on the Merits in Support of the Petitioner, L. A. Nixon.

36 **The bill passed:** Nixon's first case was being retried in El Paso (the Supreme Court had denied the lower court) when this took place in 1927. It appears that Nixon's lawyer, Knollenberg, and the NAACP had not yet agreed on a strategy for further court battles when Knollenberg began to execute his strategy by having Nixon send letters to all the members of the state Democratic Executive Committee (who had voted to pass the whites-only resolution) threatening a suit. According to Nixon's biographer, Conrey Bryson, the NAACP got on board quickly and took on another case (with Knollenberg at the helm). Bryson, *Dr. Lawrence A. Nixon and the White Primary*, 51–54.

37 **circuit court writing:** From Circuit Court ruling quoted in Supreme Court of the United States, October Term, 1931, No. 265, L. A. Nixon, Petitioner, v. James Condon and C. H. Kolle, Respondents, On Writ of

Certiorari to the United States Circuit Court of Appeals for the Fifth Circuit, Opinion of the Court, 4.

38 **The supporting brief written:** Supreme Court of the United States, October Term, 1931, No. 265, L. A. Nixon, Petitioner, v. James Condon and C. H. Kolle, Respondents, On Writ of Certiorari to the United States Circuit Court of Appeals for the Fifth Circuit, Petition for Certiorari Filed July 30, 1931, Certiorari Granted Oct. 19, 1931.

39 **"As to that":** Supreme Court of the United States, October Term, 1931, No. 265, L. A. Nixon, Petitioner, v. James Condon and C. H. Kolle, Respondents, On Writ of Certiorari to the United States Circuit Court of Appeals for the Fifth Circuit [May 2, 1932], From the opinion delivered by Mr. Justice Cardoza.

40 **"any rights guaranteed by the Fourteenth":** 295 U.S. 45, 55 S.Ct. 622, 79 L.Ed. 1292, Grovey v. Townsend, No. 563. Argued Mar. 11, 1935. Decided Apr. 1, 1935. Opinion of the Court, https://www.law.cornell.edu/supremecourt/text/295/45.

40 **He responded:** Bryson, *Dr. Lawrence A. Nixon and the White Primary*, 73.

40 **"white" race:** All the more surprising as the U.S. Census had only just begun to *stop* classifying Latinos as "white," by adding the category "Mexican" for the 1930 census.

42 **On April 3, 1944, the court decided:** Found in the court's opinion, 321 U.S. 649, 64 S.Ct. 757. 88 L.Ed. 987, Smith v. Allwright, Election Judge, et al., No. 51. Reargued Jan. 12, 1944. Decided Apr. 3, 1944. As Amended June 12, 1944, https://www.law.cornell.edu/supremecourt/text/321/649.

42 **290 African Americans:** Bryson, *Dr. Lawrence A. Nixon and the White Primary*, 74.

43 **Nixon wrote, "The negro in El Paso":** *El Paso Times*, Oct. 24, 1999,

cited in Bryson, *Dr. Lawrence A. Nixon and the White Primary*, 79, https://www.newspapers.com/newspage/432211752/.

3: COOKE COUNTY

53   **A line of his came to mind:** Truman Library Institute, "Truman Quotes," https://www.trumanlibraryinstitute.org/truman/truman -quotes/page/2/#:~:text=AMERICA%20WAS%20BUILT%20ON%20 COURAGE,DO%20THE%20JOB%20AT%20HAND.&text=I%20 don't%20believe%20that,difficult%20that%20war%20is%20inevitable.

54   **The Voting Rights Act:** U.S. Department of Justice, Civil Rights Division, "Jurisdictions Previously Covered by Section 5," https://www .justice.gov/crt/jurisdictions-previously-covered-section-5 (accessed Feb. 16, 2022).

57   **Facing north:** Megan Gray-Hatfield, "Monumental Decision: County Commissioners Vote to Leave Confederate Statue Where It Stands," *Gainesville Register*, Aug. 17, 2020, https://www.gainesvilleregister .com/news/local_news/monumental-decision-county-commissioners -vote-to-leave-confederate-statue-where-it-stands/article_17722270 -e0d5-11ea-b021-93fe5d308df6.html.

57   **From a dedication:** Found at the Lee Family Digital Archive, https:// leefamilyarchive.org/reference/books/shepherd/05.html.

57   **As I would later learn:** The history summarized in the next few paragraphs can be found in Richard B. McCaslin, "Great Hanging at Gainesville," Texas State Historical Association, 1976, https://www .tshaonline.org/handbook/entries/great-hanging-at-gainesville (accessed Apr. 27, 2022).

58   **It is worth noting:** A detailed history of the Dakota War can be found at "The U.S.-Dakota War of 1862," www.usdakotawar.org. For more detail on Lincoln and General George Sibley's mass hanging, see https://www.usdakotawar.org/history/aftermath/trials-hanging.

59   **a memorial in 2014:** Abby Rapoport, "How Do You Memorialize a Mob?," *Texas Observer*, Nov. 17, 2014, https://www.texasobserver.org /great-hanging-gainesville/.

4: PECOS COUNTY

72   **Outstanding Rural Scholar Recognition Program:** This program of the Texas Department of Agriculture provides forgivable matching fund loans to help rural communities fund the education of their own health care professionals. See https://www.texasagriculture.gov/GrantsServices /RuralEconomicDevelopment/StateOfficeofRuralHealth/ProgramList /ORS.aspx.

73   **Compounding these challenges:** Bonnie Petrie, "Texas Primary Care Doctor Shortage Spikes During the Pandemic; Rural Texans Hit Hardest," Texas Public Radio, Nov. 17, 2021, https://www.keranews .org/2021-11-17/texas-primary-care-doctor-shortage-spikes-during -the-pandemic-rural-texans-hit-hardest.

76   **she saw the benefit:** "Oveta Culp Hobby," Rice University, https:// digitalprojects.rice.edu/wrc/Secretary-Hobby-HEW/exhibits/show /secretary-of-health--education/introduction.

76   **it was a man:** Wilbur J. Cohen, "Reflections on the Enactment of Medicaid and Medicare," *Health Care Financing Review* (December 1985) (Suppl.): 3–11, https://www.ncbi.nlm.nih.gov/pmc/articles /PMC4195078/#b5-hcfr-85-supp-003.

76   **766,000 people:** Laura Harker, "Closing the Coverage Gap a Critical Step for Advancing Health and Economic Justice," Center on Budget and Policy Priorities, Oct. 4, 2021, https://www.cbpp.org/research /health/closing-the-coverage-gap-a-critical-step-for-advancing-health -and-economic-justice.

81   **Within five years:** Joe Petrie, "Sun Metro Shines over El Paso," *Mass Transit*, Feb. 11, 2014, https://www.masstransitmag.com/home

/article/11288720/el-pasos-mass-transit-system-overhauls-itself-as
-a-leader.

82 **The ordinance passed:** Melissa Del Bosque, "The Straight and Narrow-
Minded," *Texas Observer*, Apr. 30, 2012, https://www.texasobserver.org
/the-straight-narrow-minded/.

82 **seven hundred thousand dollars in personal legal:** Aileen B. Flores,
"Cook, Brown Reach Settlement in Recall Attempt," *El Paso Times*, May
9, 2016, https://www.elpasotimes.com/story/news/local/community/2016
/05/09/cook-brown-reach-settlement-recall-attempt/84161202/.

5: LA SALLE COUNTY

88 **Often against great resistance:** "LBJ in Cotulla," LBJ Museum, San
Marcos, Texas, https://lbjmuseum.com/lbj-in-cotulla/ (accessed Feb.
21, 2022), and Melissa Block, "LBJ Carried Poor Texas Town with Him
in Civil Rights Fight," *All Things Considered*, NPR, Apr. 11, 2014, https://
www.npr.org/2014/04/11/301820334/lbj-carried-cotulla-with-him-in
-civil-rights-fight (accessed Feb. 21, 2022).

88 **Johnson spoke to a joint session of Congress:** From Johnson's March
15, 1965, address to Congress to push for the Voting Rights Act. See
Public Papers of the Presidents of the United States: Lyndon B. Johnson (1965, Book 1), Jan. 1 to May 31, 1965, GS 4.113:965/BK.1, available for download at https://www.govinfo.gov/app/details/PPP-1965
-book1.

92 **the largest in the United States:** According to a report commis-
sioned by the City of Arlington, "Arlington, Texas is the largest city
in the United States of America without a public transportation system for its residents." From Briana Ousley et al., "An Evaluation
of Public Transportation in Arlington, Texas," College of Architecture, Planning and Public Affairs, University of Texas at Arlington,
Nov. 30, 2020, https://rc.library.uta.edu/uta-ir/bitstream/handle/10106
/29605/Evaluation%20of%20Public%20Transportation%20in%20

Arlington%2C%20Texas%20-%20Report.pdf?sequence=1&is
Allowed=y.

92   **Alisa also brought:** From 2013 to 2019, the Arlington Police Department used more force per arrest than 85 percent of police forces, and 62 percent of the people killed by police were Black (54 percent) and Hispanic (8 percent). See https://policescorecard.org/.

96   **The 1975 extension:** Suzanne Gamboa, "For Latinos, 1965 Voting Rights Act Impact Came a Decade Later," NBC News, Aug. 6, 2015, https://www.nbcnews.com/news/latino/latinos-1965-voting-rights -act-impact-came-decade-later-n404936.

97   **"I know firsthand":** Ari Berman, "The Lost Promise of the Voting Rights Act," *The Atlantic*, Aug. 5, 2015, https://www.theatlantic.com /politics/archive/2015/08/give-us-the-ballot-expanding-the-voting -rights-act/399128/. Excerpted from Berman's book, *Give Us the Ballot: The Modern Struggle for Voting Rights in America* (Macmillan, 2015).

99   **As Berman writes:** Ibid.

100   **smaller towns like Cotulla:** As of this writing, there are no licensed private schools in Cotulla or surrounding La Salle County.

103   **"I never thought then":** "LBJ Speech Before Congress on Voting Rights," Mar. 15, 1965, Miller Center, University of Virginia.

104   **At Welhausen that day:** "LBJ Remarks at the Welhausen Elementary School, Cotulla, Texas," Nov. 7, 1966, UC Santa Barbara American Presidency Project, https://www.presidency.ucsb.edu/documents /remarks-the-welhausen-elementary-school-cotulla-texas (accessed Feb. 20, 2022).

6: FORT BEND COUNTY

107   **man named Reginald Moore:** Michael Hardy, "Blood and Sugar," *Texas Monthly,* Jan. 2017, https://www.texasmonthly.com/articles/sugar -land-slave-convict-labor-history/.

NOTES

108   **Colonel Edward H. Cunningham:** Amy E. Dase, "Hell-Hole on the Brazos: A Historic Resources Study of Central State Farm, Fort Bend County, Texas," Principal Investigators: Amy E. Dase and Douglas K. Boyd, Technical Reports, no. 70, Submitted to Berg-Oliver Associates, Inc., Houston, Texas, by Prewitt and Associates, Inc., Cultural Resources Services, Austin, Texas, Sep. 2004, https://int.nyt.com/data/documenthelper/151-hell-hole-on-the-brazos/f39a6d5be573318f1fa3/optimized/full.pdf.

108   **on June 19, 1865:** This took place almost two and a half years after the Emancipation Proclamation abolished slavery. Texas's enslaved population had no previous knowledge of this and did not know they had been freed.

109   **enslaved Texans free:** Texas was the last Confederate state to hold the constitutional convention required to fully reenter the Union. At that time, it followed all the requirements but one: with almost no dissent, the convention barred Black Texans from voting or holding public office and refused to ratify the Fourteenth Amendment. Symbolic as these actions were, they show the determination with which Texans wanted to hold on to the old ways. See Adrien D. Ivan, "Masters No More: Abolition and Texas Planters, 1860–1890," Ph.D. dissertation, University of North Texas, 2010.

109   **the financial cornerstone:** Charles S. Potts, "The Convict Labor System of Texas," *Annals of the American Academy of Political and Social Science* 21, Problems in Charities and Corrections (May 1903): 84–95.

109   **eager for the cheap labor:** Hardy, "Blood and Sugar."

109   **Convicts worked "barelegged":** Brooke A. Lewis, "'Human Lives Were Not of Value': African-American Remains Awaken History of Convict-Leasing System," *Houston Chronicle*, https://www.houstonchronicle.com/news/houston-texas/houston/article/Human-lives-were-not-of-value-13518549.php.

109   **Whippings were common:** "Report of the Penitentiary Investigating Committee," Texas House of Representatives, Aug. 1910, 7, https://lrl.texas.gov/scanned/interim/31/31_PenitInvestPartI.pdf.

NOTES

110   **A visiting doctor:** Dase, "Hell-Hole on the Brazos."

110   **The punishing conditions:** Ibid.

111   **But evil as it may have been:** Ibid.

111   **The investigative committee:** Texas State Library and Archives Commission, "Fear, Force, and Leather—The Texas Prison System's First Hundred Years, 1848–1948," 1, https://www.tsl.texas.gov /exhibits/prisons/scandal/page1.html.

111   **six years after the investigation:** Ibid., 2

112   **"On the women's farm":** George Waverley Briggs, "Treatment of These Women Is Inhuman," *San Antonio Daily Express,* Dec. 13, 1908, 21.

113   **"We recommend":** Ibid.

113   **claimed an estimated:** According to author Robert Perkinson, between 1866 (the inception of the leasing system) and 1912 (when the last contracts expired), 3,558 prisoners lost their lives, the majority from "unnatural" causes. See Robert Perkinson, *Texas Tough: The Rise of America's Prison Empire* (Henry Holt, 2010), 128.

114   **first Black sheriff:** Melissa Maluski, "Blog: First Black Sheriff in the U.S. Was Elected in Southeast Texas in 1869," 2022, https://www .county.org/Blog/Blog-First-Black-sheriff-elected-SE-Texas-1869.

115   **By the summer of 1888:** Leslie Ann Lovett, "The Jaybird-Woodpecker War: Reconstruction and Redemption in Fort Bend County, Texas, 1869–1889," Ph.D. dissertation, Rice University, May 1994.

115   **phenomenal Black political success:** Fort Bend County was one of the largest slaveholding counties per capita in Texas, with a population that was 80 percent Black. The majority slaveholding population voted 100 percent to secede from the Union. However, these numbers created the perfect setting for postwar Black political success. Ibid.

115   **In early 1889:** Pauline Yelderman, "Jaybird-Woodpecker War," Texas State Historical Association, 1952, https://www.tshaonline.org /handbook/entries/jaybird-woodpecker-war (accessed Apr. 28, 2022).

115   **Jaybird leader:** Ned Gibson, who happened to be on the way to testify in a trial for cattle rustling. See Geni, "Jefferson Kyle Terry," https://www.geni.com/people/Kyle-Terry/6000000106254276913.

115   **Benjamin Franklin Terry:** Kenneth W. Hobbs, "Terry, Benjamin Franklin," Texas State Historical Association, 1952, https://www.tshaonline.org/handbook/entries/terry-benjamin-franklin (accessed Apr. 28, 2022).

116   **Within a year, Kyle Terry:** By Volney Gibson, the brother of the man Terry had murdered in Fort Bend. See https://www.geni.com/people/Kyle-Terry/6000000106254276913.

116   **until 1953:** 97 L.Ed. 1152, Terry et al v. Adams, et al., No. 52. Argued Jan. 16, 1953. Decided May 4, 1953. Cornell Law School Legal Information Institute, https://www.law.cornell.edu/supremecourt/text/345/461.

118   **Today, Texas holds:** Sentencing Project, "Private Prisons in the United States," Mar. 3, 2021, https://www.sentencingproject.org/publications/private-prisons-united-states/.

119   **those behind bars:** Tom Dart, "Building over History: The Prison Graveyard Buried Under a Texas Suburb," *The Guardian*, Jun. 22, 2019, https://www.theguardian.com/us-news/2019/jun/22/sugar-land-texas-95-burial-ground.

119   **The incarceration rate:** Prison Policy Initiative, "Texas Profile," https://www.prisonpolicy.org/profiles/TX.html.

122   **told the *Houston Chronicle*:** Anna Bauman, "Design Firm Seeks to 'Heal the Landscape' with Sugar Land 95 Memorial," *Houston Chronicle*, Dec. 11, 2021, https://www.houstonchronicle.com/news/houston-texas/houston/article/Design-firm-seeks-to-heal-the-landscape-16692543.php.

122   **"I was raised":** Natalie Cook Clark, "Meet Fort Bend County 'Sheriff for Everyone,' Eric Fagan," *Katy Magazine*, Mar. 1, 2021, https://www.katymagazineonline.com/post/meet-fort-bend-county-sheriff-for-everyone-eric-fagan.

NOTES

122 **"Fort Bend is the most diverse":** Brooke A. Lewis, "Fort Bend, Richmond Agree to Remove Jaybird Statue Honoring White Supremacists from Spot near City Hall," *Houston Chronicle,* Oct. 27, 2020.

7: THE BORDER, PART I

123 **The end of that once vibrant community**: For a detailed accounting of the massacre at Porvenir, see Monica Muñoz Martinez, *The Injustice Never Leaves You: Anti-Mexican Violence in Texas* (Harvard University Press, 2018), chapter 3.

124 **The cover-up was exposed:** Jasmine Aguilera, "'I Cry All the Time': A Century After 15 Mexican Men and Boys Were Massacred in Texas, Their Descendants Want Recognition," *Time,* Sep. 27, 2019, https://time.com/5682139/porvenir-massacre-descendants/.

126 **There is a mural:** Freddie Martinez, "On the Streets of El Paso and Juarez, 'Sister Cities' Art Project Pays Tribute to Border Communities," *Remezcla,* July 7, 2016, https://remezcla.com/features/culture/interview-los-dos/.

129 **Since 9/11:** Muzaffar Chishti and Jessica Bolter, "Two Decades After 9/11, National Security Focus Still Dominates U.S. Immigration System," Migration Policy Institute, Sep. 22, 2021, https://www.migrationpolicy.org/article/two-decades-after-sept-11-immigration-national-security.

129 **no additional security gains:** U.S. Government Accountability Office, "Secure Border Initiative: DHS Needs to Reconsider Its Proposed Investment in Key Technology Program," May 2010, https://www.gao.gov/products/gao-10-340.

129 **In 2021 alone:** Priscilla Alvarez, "At Least 650 Migrants Died Crossing the US-Mexico Border, the Most Since 2014, International Agency Says," CNN, Dec. 9, 2021, https://www.cnn.com/2021/12/09/politics/migrants-dying-crossing-us-mexico-border/index.html.

NOTES

129   **In 2002:** Mary Dougherty, Denise Wilson, and Amy Wu, "Immigration Enforcement Actions: 2004," Office of Immigration Statistics, Management Directorate, Homeland Security, Nov. 2005, https://www.dhs.gov/sites/default/files/publications/Enforcement_Actions_2004.pdf.

129   **In 2019, there were 977,500:** Julián Aguilar, "Border Patrol Apprehensions Dipped Last Month, but 2019 Saw a Dramatic Increase from 2018," *Texas Tribune*, Oct. 8, 2019, https://www.texastribune.org/2019/10/08/border-patrol-apprehensions-dipped-last-month-rose-2019-over-2018/.

133   **Though Trump's claims were disproven:** Amy Gardner, "Inaccurate Claims of Noncitizen Voting in Texas Reflect a Growing Trend in Republican States," *Washington Post*, Feb. 6, 2019, https://www.washingtonpost.com/politics/inaccurate-claims-of-noncitizen-voting-in-texas-reflect-a-growing-trend-in-republican-states/2019/02/06/af376fb0-2994-11e9-b011-d8500644dc98_story.html.

133   **Cruz said the bill:** Brandon Mulder, "Fact-Check: Would Democrats' Voting Rights Bill 'Register Millions of Illegal Aliens to Vote'?," *Austin American-Statesman*, May 14, 2021, https://www.statesman.com/story/news/politics/politifact/2021/05/14/would-democrats-voting-rights-bill-register-millions-illegal-aliens-vote-voting-laws-ted-cruz/5090859001/.

135   **In 1915, El Paso:** Aaron Martinez, "100 Years After El Paso Becomes the First in the Nation to Outlaw Pot, Debate Remains the Same," *El Paso Times*, June 2, 2015, https://www.elpasotimes.com/story/news/local/2015/06/02/100-years-after-el-paso-becomes-first-city/31234363/.

135   **One editorialist wrote:** Rebecca Onion, "America's Lost History of Border Violence," *Slate*, May 5, 2016, https://slate.com/news-and-politics/2016/05/texas-finally-begins-to-grapple-with-its-ugly-history-of-border-violence-against-mexican-americans.html.

NOTES

135   **Texans of Mexican descent:** Testimony of Monica Muñoz Martinez, Ph.D., Stanley J. Bernstein Assistant Professor of American Studies and Ethnic Studies, Brown University, Before Committee on the Judiciary Subcommittee on the Immigration and Citizenship, Hearing on "Oversight of the Trump Administration's Border Policies and the Relationship Between Anti-Immigrant Rhetoric and Domestic Terrorism," Sep. 6, 2019, https://www.congress.gov/116/meeting/house /109889/witnesses/HHRG-116-JU01-Wstate-MunozMartinezM -20190906.pdf.

135   **these fears were confirmed:** Don M. Coerver, "Plan of San Diego," Texas State Historical Association, June 1, 1995, https://www.tshaonline .org/handbook/entries/plan-of-san-diego (accessed Jan. 10, 2022).

135   **Plan de San Diego:** Ibid. The plan was a revolutionary manifesto drafted and signed in January 1915 and named for the South Texas town of San Diego. It was actually written in a jail cell in Monterrey, Nuevo León, Mexico. Feb. 20, 1915, was the day the revolution would begin, but federal and state officials came into possession of the manifesto when, on January 24, local authorities in McAllen, Texas, arrested one of the leaders of the plot, Basilio Ramos Jr.

136   **including Longoria:** "Bazan Ranch Cemetery," Cemeteries of Texas website, http://www.cemeteries-of-tx.com/Etx/Hidalgo/Cemetery /bazan.htm.

136   **despite the public nature:** Testimony of Monica Muñoz Martinez.

137   **Counties that saw extrajudicial executions:** Brett W. Pelham, Ph.D., Montgomery College, Georgetown University. Forthcoming book, working title *Understanding and Reducing Systemic Racism*, (Oxford University Press: 2022).

137   **the "Loyalty Rangers":** Rusty Bloxom, "The Texas Rangers and World War I," Texas Ranger Hall of Fame and Museum, https://www .texasranger.org/texas-ranger-museum/history/general-texas-ranger -history/the-texas-rangers-and-world-war-i/.

NOTES

137   **One political observer noted:** Refusing to Forget, "The History of Racial Violence on the Mexico-Texas Border," https://refusingtoforget .org/the-history/.

8: THE BORDER, PART 2

139   **In 1917, U.S. authorities:** David Dorado Romo, *Ringside Seat to a Revolution: An Underground Cultural History of El Paso and Juárez: 1893–1923* (Cinco Puntos Press, 2005).

139   **Carmelita Torres:** Ibid.

141   **If the goal was:** Shawn Lay, *War, Revolution and the Ku Klux Klan* (Texas Western Press, 1985), 81.

141   **roughly 80 percent:** Extrapolated from 1920 U.S. Census data and estimates provided in Arnoldo De León, ed., *War Along the Border: The Mexican Revolution and Tejano Communities* (Texas A&M University Press, 2012), https://www.google.com/books/edition/War_along_the_Border /RfUWJHNxFUEC?hl=en&gbpv=1&dq=racial+breakdown+of+El+Pa so+TX+population+statistics+1920&pg=PA151&printsec=frontcover.

141   **A front for a growing:** Lay, *War, Revolution and the Ku Klux Klan*, 95.

141   **It also publicized:** Ibid., 100.

141   **Klan-led voting irregularities:** "The Election Case of George E. B. Peddy v. Earle B. Mayfield of Texas (1925)," United States Senate, https://www.senate.gov/about/origins-foundations/electing-appointing -senators/contested-senate-elections/103Peddy_Mayfield.htm.

141   **The "imperial wizard":** Lisa C. Maxwell, "Evans, Hiram Wesley (1881–1966)," Texas State Historical Association, Jan. 1, 1995, https:// www.tshaonline.org/handbook/entries/evans-hiram-wesley (accessed May 6, 2022).

142   **the county treasurer boasted:** Lay, *War, Revolution and the Ku Klux Klan*, 136.

NOTES

142 **killing nine:** Will Guzmán, *Civil Rights in the Texas Borderlands: Dr. Lawrence Nixon and Black Activism* (University of Illinois Press, 2015), 70.

142 **The Klan's Good Government League:** Lay, *War, Revolution and the Ku Klux Klan*, 120.

143 **A Houston Klansman:** Guzmán, *Civil Rights in the Texas Borderlands*, 70.

144 **They created:** Christopher Hooks, "What If They Held an Election and Everyone Came?," *Texas Monthly*, Nov. 2020, https://www.texasmonthly.com/news-politics/voter-suppression-texas-history/.

144 **the Texas secretary of state:** Andrew Weber, "Texas' Top Election Official Says Nearly 100,000 Voters Aren't U.S. Citizens," KUT.org, Jan. 25, 2019, https://www.kut.org/texas/2019-01-25/texas-top-election-official-says-nearly-100-000-voters-arent-u-s-citizens.

144 **the League of United Latin American Citizens:** Alexa Ura, "Texas Will End Its Botched Voter Citizenship Review and Rescind Its List of Flagged Voters," *Texas Tribune*, Apr. 26, 2019, https://www.texastribune.org/2019/04/26/texas-voting-rights-groups-win-settlement-secretary-of-state/.

144 **County registrars:** Michael Hardy, "Texas Election Officials Went Looking for Illegal Voters. They Found Some U.S. Citizens," *Texas Monthly*, Dec. 9, 2021, https://www.texasmonthly.com/news-politics/texas-voter-roll-non-citizens/.

145 **In November 2020:** Paul J. Weber, "Texas' Patrick Offers Reward as Trump Makes Unfounded Claims," Associated Press, Nov. 11, 2020, https://www.nbcdfw.com/news/politics/decision-2020/texas-patrick-offers-reward-as-trump-makes-unfounded-claims/2476392/ (accessed Jan. 18, 2022); Lauren McGaughy, "Texas Lt. Gov. Dan Patrick's First Voter Fraud Bounty Goes to a PA Democrat," *Dallas Morning News*, Oct. 21, 2021, https://www.nbcdfw.com/news/local/texas-news/texas-lt-gov-dan-patrick-has-paid-his-first-voter-fraud-bounty-to-a-pa-democrat/2779671/.

146   **Alvaro Meno:** Bill Hutchinson, Aaron Katersky, and Josh Margolin,
       "Alleged Shooter Cased El Paso Walmart Before Rampage That Killed
       22: Law Enforcement Officials," ABC News, Aug. 5, 2019, https://
       abcnews.go.com/US/death-toll-rises-22-el-paso-shooting-victims
       /story?id=64780680.

147   **"When Mexico sends":** Fabiola Cineas, "Donald Trump Is the Ac-
       celerant," *Vox,* Jan. 9, 2021, https://www.vox.com/21506029/trump
       -violence-tweets-racist-hate-speech.

147   **investigation by *USA Today*:** John Fritze, "Trump Used Words Like
       'Invasion' and 'Killer' to Discuss Immigrants at Rallies 500 Times,"
       USA Today, Aug. 8, 2019, https://www.usatoday.com/story/news
       /politics/elections/2019/08/08/trump-immigrants-rhetoric-criticized
       -el-paso-dayton-shootings/1936742001/.

148   **At another rally:** "Trump Laughs Off 'Shoot Them' Remark About
       Migrants at Florida Rally," Youtube, May 19, 2019, https://www
       .youtube.com/watch?v=jt5dzCd1pJQ.

148   **Greg Abbott mailed:** Brianna Sacks, "The Texas Governor Called on
       Supporters to 'Defend' Against Immigrants the Day Before the El Paso
       Massacre," *Daily Beast,* Aug. 23, 2019, https://www.buzzfeednews
       .com/article/briannasacks/greg-abbott-governor-letter-defend-texas
       -el-paso.

149   **Dan Patrick appeared:** Justin Baragona, "Texas Lt. Guv Spews Racist
       'Great Replacement' Theory on Fox: 'A Revolution Has Begun,'" *Daily
       Beast,* Sep. 17, 2021, https://www.thedailybeast.com/texas-lt-gov-dan
       -patrick-spews-racist-great-replacement-theory-on-fox-news?ref=scroll.

9: OVERCOMING

159   **"Being brown":** Alexander Wolff, "The Barrio Boys," *Sports Illustrated,*
       June 27, 2011, https://vault.si.com/vault/2011/06/27/the-barrio-boys.

NOTES

160   **The school's registrar:** Darren Meritz, "2004: 50 Years of Integration," *El Paso Times,* Sep. 4, 2014 (originally published May 17, 2004), https://www.elpasotimes.com/story/news/history/blogs/tales-from -the-morgue/2014/09/04/2004/31509811/.

161   **among them:** University of Texas at El Paso online encyclopedia, https:// ucweb.utep.edu/_uploaded/encyclopedia-temp/pages/NAACP.html.

162   **R. E. Thomason, the same judge:** "1957: R. E. Thomason Gives Oath of Office to Raymond Telles," *El Paso Times,* July 3, 2012 (originally published Apr. 12, 1957), https://www.elpasotimes.com/story/news /history/blogs/tales-from-the-morgue/2012/07/03/1957-re-thomason -gives-oath-of-office-to-raymond-telles/31510175/.

162   **asked by President John F. Kennedy:** Jose Maria Herrera, "Telles, Raymond Lorenzo, Jr. (1915–2013)," Texas State Historical Association, Sep. 2, 2019, https://www.tshaonline.org/handbook/entries /telles-raymond-lorenzo-jr (accessed Jan. 28, 2022).

162   **Williams had grown up:** Chris Roberts, "2010: Williams Led El Paso on Path to Desegregation," *El Paso Times,* May 25, 2017 (originally published Nov. 14, 2010), https://www.elpasotimes.com/story /news/local/el-paso/2017/05/25/bert-williams-91-champion-people /102168148/.

164   **"We went inside":** Ibid.

164   **Williams and Seitsinger:** Ibid.

165   **Nixon's wife, Drusilla:** Will Guzmán, "Border Physician: The Life of Lawrence A. Nixon, 1883–1966," Ph.D. dissertation, University of Texas at El Paso, Dec. 2010, 213, https://digitalcommons.utep.edu /open_etd/2495.

166   **But Rupp had:** Jesse Washington, "Kentucky Must Reckon with the Full Meaning of Adolph Rupp," Andscape, Aug. 7, 2020, https:// theundefeated.com/features/kentucky-must-reckon-with-the-full -meaning-of-adolph-rupp/.

NOTES

169 **State of the Union address:** Steve Benson, "Why Trump's Lie About El Paso, Texas, Is So Important," MSNBC, Feb. 11, 2019, https://www.msnbc.com/rachel-maddow-show/why-trumps-lie-about-el-paso-texas-so-important-msna1193651.

10: FORWARD

173 **new district voting maps:** James Barragán, Abby Livingston, and Carla Astudillo, "Texas Reduces Black and Hispanic Majority Congressional Districts in Proposed Map, Despite People of Color Fueling Population Growth," *Texas Tribune*, Sep. 27, 2021, https://www.texastribune.org/2021/09/24/texas-congressional-redistricting/.

174 **old-school voter suppression:** Cayla Harris, "DOJ Sues Texas, Claiming New Political Maps Discriminate Against Minority Voters," *Houston Chronicle*, Dec. 6, 2021, https://www.houstonchronicle.com/politics/texas/article/justice-department-sues-texas-redistricting-maps-16679772.php.

175 **voting rights scholar:** Ari Berman, "Texas Is the Hardest State to Vote In. It Could Soon Get Much Harder," *Mother Jones*, July 8, 2021, https://www.motherjones.com/politics/2021/07/texas-is-the-hardest-state-to-vote-in-it-could-soon-get-much-harder/.

175 **eighty-seven thousand Texans:** As of March 2022.

175 **Ken Paxton:** Benjamin Wermund, "Ken Paxton at Trump's D.C. Rally: 'We Will Not Quit Fighting,'" *Houston Chronicle*, Jan. 6, 2021, https://www.houstonchronicle.com/politics/texas/article/Paxton-Trump-DC-rally-election-2020-georgia-15850073.php.

177 **The GOP officials:** Teo Armus and Derek Hawkins, "Video Shows Texas GOP Official Seeking 'Army' of Volunteers to Monitor Polls in Mostly Black and Hispanic Houston Precincts," *Washington Post*, Apr. 8, 2021, https://www.washingtonpost.com/nation/2021/04/08/texas-voting-gop-poll-watchers/.

178 **"an assault on democracy":** Ben Leonard, "'Assault on Democracy': Biden Torches Texas Voting Bill," *Politico*, May 29, 2021, https://www.politico.com/news/2021/05/29/biden-texas-voting-restrictions-491415.

179 **"One thing the Senate":** Sam Levine, "'Time Is Running Out': Can Congress Pass a Voting Rights Bill After Months of Failure?," *The Guardian*, Dec. 6, 2021, https://www.theguardian.com/us-news/2021/dec/06/voting-rights-biden-democrats-voting-rights-legislation.

179 **It's a tall order:** Adam Jentleson, "Will Biden Join the Fight for Voting Rights?," *New York Times*, Aug. 29, 2021, https://www.nytimes.com/2021/08/29/opinion/biden-voting-rights.html.

EPILOGUE

182 **The Associated Press reported:** Bud Kennedy/Associated Press, "Woman Recalls When Juneteenth Celebrations Drew Racist Mobs," *Washington Times*, Oct. 26, 2015, https://www.washingtontimes.com/news/2015/oct/26/woman-recalls-when-juneteenth-celebrations-drew-ra/.

182 **"The fact that it happened":** Bud Kennedy, "She Was 12 When Whites Smashed Her Home. At 93, Opal Lee Leads a Walk for Unity," *Fort Worth Star Telegram*, July 25, 2021, https://www.star-telegram.com/news/politics-government/article243442951.html.

183 **Opal Lee decided:** Meryl Kornfield, "Meet Opal Lee, the 94-Year-Old Activist Who Marched for Miles to Make Juneteenth a Federal Holiday," *Washington Post*, June 19, 2021, https://www.washingtonpost.com/history/2021/06/19/juneteenth-opal-lee/.

183 **In his remarks:** "Remarks by President Biden at the Signing of the Juneteenth National Independence Day Act," June 17, 2021, https://www.whitehouse.gov/briefing-room/speeches-remarks/2021/06/17/remarks-by-president-biden-at-signing-of-the-juneteenth-national-independence-day-act/.

184 **Opal Lee agreed:** Kennedy, "She Was 12 When Whites Smashed Her Home."

About the Author

Beto O'Rourke is a fourth-generation Texan, born and raised in El Paso, where he has served as a small business owner, a city council representative, and a member of Congress. He founded Powered by People, a Texas-based organization that works to expand democracy and produce Democratic victories through voter registration and direct voter engagement. Beto is married to Amy O'Rourke, and together they are raising Ulysses, Molly, and Henry in El Paso's historic Sunset Heights.